"Stan is a gifted individual who can take a routine of an interesting story that will challenge your way of thinking. He lives ... and is an inspiration to all who cross his path."
Tim Miller,
Partner and Director of Marketing & Advertising,
La-Z-Boy Furniture Galleries of Greater Vancouver

"Stan's word pictures take you on a warm and friendly journey to beautiful places that are actually just over the next tree line on familiar trails. Reading them is like taking a stroll side by side with someone you've always known. Your surroundings melt away as you trek along deep in thought—and you are sure you detect a mischievous glint in Stan's eye. You'll want the stories to keep flowing and flowing."
Steve Farrant,
Retired Senior Hospital Executive, Paris, Ontario

"Well done, Stan, for taking what many men consider a barrier (vulnerability) and converting it into an emotional drawbridge, as you urge us to cross over with you and experience real life! Thank you for bringing us along on your journey."
Michael and Adele Robert,
The Crossroads, Panajachel, Guatemala

"Stan Hindmarsh's reflections and photographs are a shared feast, offering a hard-won glimpse into the goodness at the heart of life. Endlessly curious, he immerses himself in whatever comes—family, friends and the natural world—then opens a window into his own inner thoughts and beliefs. Typically those willing to get out and plumb the deep recesses of life as Stan does don't take time to write about it. A lot of heart and life lived have gone into these writings, and it shows."
Melody Goetz,
Chief Cultural Officer, Hallmark Communities

"It is a true blessing and an excellent adventure to share this 'walk home' with a good friend like Stan. He has a totally different view of the smallest things. He has opened many doors into people's lives and stayed a while to understand them and care for them."
Ron Martens, Managing Principal,
Keystone Architecture & Planning Ltd.

"Stan writes how friends should communicate. This is what friends do for each other."
Vern Heidebrecht, Pastor Emeritus,
Northview Community Church, Abbotsford, B.C.

Crossroads...

Conversations
on the way Home

by Stan Hindmarsh

Hardy

Thanks for your friendship and encouragement. Thanks for reading these stories about *our* journey "home." We have some pretty good company along the path :)

Blessings
Stan

"Teach us to realize the brevity of life, so that we may grow in wisdom." Psalms 90:12

Mill Lake Books

Mill Lake Books
Abbotsford, BC
Canada
www.coggins.ca

Printed and distributed by IngramSpark

Cover design and layout by Dean Tjepkema

Unless otherwise noted, all Bible quotations are taken from the Holy
Bible, New Living Translation, copyright © 1996, 2004, 2015 by Tyndale
House Foundation. Used by permission of Tyndale House Publishers Inc.,
Carol Stream, Illinois 60188. All rights reserved.

Bible quotations marked KJV are taken from the King James Version.

Bible quotations marked NIV are taken from the Holy Bible, New International
Version®, NIV® Copyright ©1973, 1978, 1984, 2011 by Biblica, Inc.® Used
by permission. All rights reserved worldwide.

Bible quotations marked NLV are taken from the New Life Version Copyright
© 1969 by Christian Literature International.

Unless otherwise noted, the photos in this book are by Stan Hindmarsh.

The front cover photo is used, with permission,
from iStock.com/weerapatkiatdumrong

ISBN: 978-0-9951983-1-9

Contents

Foreword

"What are you discussing so intently
as you walk along?" – Luke 24:17

"As they sat down to eat, he took
the bread and blessed it...Suddenly,
their eyes were opened, and
they recognized him."
– Luke 24:29-30

Why does one record the passage of time? It might be a secret diary, a contemplative journal, a blog of carefully considered musings, marks chiseled into a prison wall, or just penciled notes on a kitchen calendar—but we all do it. We all seem to recognize that our lives proceed from a beginning to an end, and in between there is the search for meaning and purpose, something special, something unique. Of course, the day by day of our lives is written in codified records and innumerable databases. These detail the facts and figures. In our current age, there is so much stored electronic information on each of us that the narrative of our lives could be recited in a mechanical monotone. But that would tell little about who we are.

This book, *Crossroads...Conversations on the way Home*, is not an autobiography. Indeed, it does relate some personal narratives of Stan Hindmarsh's life, his observations, emotions, and probing thoughts. But it is more than that. It is a book of conversations, a dialogue of sorts with his family, his friends, and his God. Through the vignettes recounted in these pages, we are invited into a relationship with Stan as he explores the significance of his family, friends, and faith. We journey with him as he finds meaning, personal significance, and a profoundly deep yet simple purpose in it all. Like life, the stories are ordinary and inspiring at the same time. They encompass all of life from the mundane to the mystical, the sacred to the silly. Stan shares his life openly and honestly. It is his gift, given to those for whom he cares, as well as others who may happen upon this book and, reading it, discover the author is a friend.

I count myself a friend of Stan and his family. It is a blessing to have shared time with him along the road. Often our journey together has been like that of the two disciples on the road to Emmaus, who discovered that Jesus was traveling and conversing with them. We, too, have traveled together and talked of troubles and triumphs. And, like the two disciples, in the process of our conversation, our hearts were stirred, and we were drawn deeper into a relationship with Him. As those disciples observed in Luke 24:32, "Didn't our hearts burn within us as he talked with us on the road?" In those precious times with Stan, as we wept and laughed about how God had led us in ways that we could not have imagined, our lives were changed.

This book is not really about Stan or his life, as interesting as they are. It is not so much about events or even the author's perceptions, as interesting and insightful as they are. It is about life, all muddled together, full of mistakes and mishaps, fear and boredom, moments of breath-stopping exhilaration and moments of heart-numbing hopelessness.

In the end, when silence becomes our only language, when memories stand still and are mounted like photographs on the wall, it is then that we close our eyes and are drawn to the conversations. In those times, life will have dimensions not measured in days, but in the depth of the sharing of our hearts and minds.

The passage of time provides the backdrop for our stories, the lives we give as our offering. First, we surrender our self-importance to our Creator, our Savior and Sustainer, without whom we are irretrievably lost. Our words become expressions of endless gratitude. And, second, we gladly give our lives day by day, hour by hour, to those we love. Meager though they may be, our stories, our journeys, and our conversations express our love and all we have to give.

Anyone who reads this book will participate in the conversation, the journey on the way home. The conversation may bring us to our knees or lift us to dizzying heights. But surely our hearts will burn, and we will be blessed.

Bob Kuhn, President
Trinity Western University

Introduction: Conversations on the way Home

"We spend our years as a tale that is told."
– Psalm 90:9 KJV

"If history were written in the form of stories,
it would never be forgotten."
– Rudyard Kipling

As a child, I remember sitting at my grandparents' dining room table, mesmerized as Grandpa told us stories. Some of those stories I remember to this day. Grandpa had a strong connection not only to the physical world around him, but more importantly to God, who brought it all together for him. The many hours he spent in the prairie fields of Saskatchewan and the long winters he spent tending the cattle on their mixed farm provided him with rich stories to pass on to us.

It took many years before I started to slow down and listen to the world around me as he did. I wonder if the saying "When the student is ready, the teacher will come" applied to me. Busyness of life was necessary. But, at some point in time, I fell in love with so much of what I would easily have passed by in earlier years. I realized that, as a result of my inability to slow myself down, I had missed much beauty and love in my life.

Over twenty years ago, I started writing some thoughts down in journals that are now lined up on a bookshelf. To my surprise, I discovered that I actually enjoyed writing. I had never discovered that in all my years of formal schooling—and there were plenty of those. But the school of life has taught me much, and the joy of writing has been one of many surprises.

As I journaled, I started mining thoughts a little more deeply and discovered a great treasure. As I wrote my thoughts down, these ideas pulled me deeper into my own spiritual journey, and I was often surprised by the joy that came with reflection. These meanderings drew me closer to God and His unfathomable love for me. To know that God loves us unconditionally is easy to say, but for me it was a lesson long in the learning.

This collection of stories represents some of those reflections. They are meant to be read as "conversations" over a cup of coffee, preferably in the morning. Morning is when most of my writings were birthed—early morning, as the darkness is giving way to daybreak. Imagine us sitting together, in your choice of location, sharing life, accepting the gift of each other, discussing the lives that we have lived, listening and learning from the words spoken and not spoken.

The stories are in a random order—as conversation often happens. Seldom do we allow a theme to control our talks. When we are at peace and present in the moment, conversation flows, and discoveries are made along the way.

The stories were inspired in much the same way, as I reflected on my surroundings and as God seemed to speak to me through them. Often the setting was in places we have become very fond of—the Canadian prairies where I had my roots, a cabin in British Columbia's Cariboo region, a condo in North Vancouver, and our rural home in Mt. Lehman, close to Abbotsford, B.C. Some stories have been inspired through friendships developed within our Hallmark Retirement Communities, as well as on our numerous trips to Guatemala.

Thank you for choosing to read these stories. Please feel free to contact me with your own stories. Often we find it easier to listen to the stories of others, while discounting our own. I think we weaken community by doing so.

Thank you to the many people have allowed me into their lives and have reciprocated by sharing their own stories. Your contribution to my life is immeasurable. A special thank you to the dear friends who have received e-mailed samples of these stories over the years and graciously encouraged me. They are too numerous to name, but endorsements from a few of them appear at the front of this book.

Thank you to James R. Coggins of Mill Lake Books for helping to make this book a reality.

Thank you to Bob Kuhn for writing the Foreword, which moved me deeply. He has been a good friend and has provided me great counsel in life.

Thank you to my family—my Mom, a consummate writer, my Dad, always an encourager, and my siblings and their families for their support in so many ways.

Thank you to our three sons and their beautiful families including several wonderful grandchildren, who appear at various places in the pages of this book. You are among my closest friends.

Thank you to my wife Grace, who has suffered through reading so many of my stories, and, more importantly, lived them with me. To have shared this life with you is a greater joy than I ever could have imagined. How many of these stories were born during our morning walks? How many of these stories grew out of ideas that you shared with me? I am so grateful that we can carry on with our journey and take the way home together.

And last, thank you to my grandpa, Frank Kroeker, for inspiring me to see the small as great, to hear the whisper as profound, and to accept God's incredible love for us.

This book is dedicated to
all of our children,
grandchildren,
and descendants.

Life is an adventure
and an incredible gift,
for which we should
offer up thanks
every day.

A Cup of Coffee

"This is what the LORD says: 'Stop at the crossroads and look around. Ask for the old, godly way, and walk in it. Travel its path, and you will find rest for your souls.'" – Jeremiah 6:16

For many years, our life has been enriched with service trips to Guatemala. Our first was in the spring of 1999 when we visited our youngest son, who was there as part of an educational program. We discovered a profound connection with many of the local people. A completely unexpected blessing came our way, as our friendships with several Mayans deepened and they graciously allowed us into their lives. Their impact on our lives was far greater than anything that we would have predicted. We inexplicably crossed paths with them in 1999, and we have tried to return at least annually ever since. We rejoice at the repeated opportunity to spend time with some of our dearest friends—both the Canadians who travel with us and those living in Guatemala.

The Panajachel area of Guatemala is a place central to most of the projects we have been connected to. On one of our early trips there, we discovered—thanks to Lonely Planet and local advice—what we think is just about the perfect cup of coffee. That discovery led to an enduring friendship with the owners of Crossroads Cafe, Mike and Adele Roberts, and their family. Subsequently, we have enjoyed many great coffee conversations there. The Bible verse Jeremiah 6:16 is displayed on a wall within.

Grace and I and many of our good friends have been back to that coffee shop as a required stop on our itinerary on over twenty trips to the area. New participants on a Conexions adventure (which is the name of our group) might wonder why the itinerary includes multiple visits to Crossroads. After one visit, most are hooked—not just by the good coffee and great service, but also by the many good conversations that take place in that tiny space on a street corner in Panajachel. Crossroads is a place where folks from many countries and backgrounds meet, take time to converse, learn from one another, and begin to travel together on their way "home."

For me, that coffee shop is a sign of something bigger and more profound, A crossroads provides an opportunity to choose another way to go. To proceed along any path requires a decision and the willingness to take a risk, as one doesn't know where that path will lead. A small step, and then another, takes one away from the comfort of the crossroads, where one had the option to turn around and retreat along the familiar path already taken. But that path may not take me home. The unknown path, ironically, seems to be the path that does lead home. It is as if something inside me has the knowledge and wisdom to long for home, a place of wholeness. It is a place of togetherness with God, who loves me unexplainably and unconditionally, a place of profound rest, adventure, and connection beyond imagination, a place where all will be well.

When I have encountered various "crossroads" in my life, they have often assured me that "home" is ahead. My crossroads encounters are personal, but there is a wise proverb that reminds me that what is most personal is often most universal.

Minus Four

"The purpose of my instruction is that all believers would be filled with love that comes from a pure heart, a clear conscience, and genuine faith." – 1 Timothy 1:5

We woke up to a beautiful morning in British Columbia's Cariboo country, our first morning there after celebrating Christmas at home in the Fraser Valley. Many times I had questioned the wisdom of extending the stress of the last month by adding a four-day trip to our summer place, called Forest Dreams, in the middle of winter. The roads on the drive up the previous day had been quite good, and the blue sky of a Cariboo morning beckoned me outside.

I put on my winter jacket and a ball cap, pulled my insulated boots on over my lined pants, and stepped out the door, drawing in a deep breath. It felt as if the fresh air was "shaking my hand," welcoming me back to this place I love. The dogs scampered out into the meadow, as excited as I was to be here. They love the snow and freedom. It felt a tad chilly, but the sun was warm on my face. For a while, I never gave the temperature another thought as I walked about, surveying the beauty.

I decided to walk over to the woodshed and gather up an armful of wood. I was surprised at how my cheeks stung a bit. I berated myself for becoming soft, having lived in the much more temperate Fraser Valley for over thirty years. The snow crunched under my boots. I noticed that one of the dogs seemed to hold up a paw, a bit surprised at the cold. I love clear, cold days and chuckled while telling the dog to get used to it.

Within half an hour, Grace joined me to take the dogs for their morning walk. She had her down-filled parka on and a scarf

wrapped around her mouth and nose. She was pretty upbeat about the beauty and stillness in this place—a good sign, as she had put out so much over the last few weeks and I had hoped that she would still have enough energy left to enjoy the next few days.

"It is minus four." Her voice was muffled under the scarf. She had looked at the thermometer on the way out of the house.

Now I was perplexed. Minus four, and I had cold cheeks. What was with that?

Even though we live in the Fraser Valley, we do see temperatures of minus four in the winter, and they seem very tolerable. At this temperature, only a strong wind should cause my cheeks to complain a bit. But the surrounding air was still. This was not good, but I resigned myself to the idea that I had become soft. After all, I am not getting any younger.

We walked up the driveway, both commenting on how cold it felt for minus four and wondering if the humidity was very high, compounding the effects of the temperature. This was a ridiculous idea because we could tell that the air was very dry. I was struggling to understand the way the cold seemed to be penetrating my body.

We got back to the house and dropped off the wood, and Grace went in to make breakfast. I did not want to go in. Our son Chris was now outside as well, so we decided to start up the snowmobiles and drive them out of the shop, ready for the day.

I had not ridden yet this year and couldn't resist taking the fastest machine out to the twenty-acre meadow for a quick run on the untouched snow. I love the sound of the engine as it revs quickly to nine thousand rpms. The snow, whipped up as I drove, fell like dust as I raced to the end of the field.

My ears were very quick to complain. I tried to convince them that it was only minus four and they should quit bellyaching. Back down the field I raced. Now my ears were really starting to bother me. I tried to pull my ball cap down over the tips. No luck. But I still wanted to go for another run up and down the field. My speed probably reached fifty miles an hour, giving me the small consolation that perhaps wind speed had now become a factor for my tingling ears.

I wanted to do a few more rounds, but my ears were really stinging, and I was quite sure that they were on the verge of frostbite. I drove back to the house a little more slowly. Putting my hands to my ears, I noticed a distinct lack of feeling along the outer edges. Oh, well.

I went into the house and had breakfast and a warm coffee, allowing everything to thaw out. I was still troubled by my apparent softness and still confused as to how that could have happened to me.

After breakfast, we had to go to the local store to pick up some groceries. In the store, they were talking about how it had dropped to minus twenty-four that night. Then the lights went on. When Grace had read the thermometer, she had read the Fahrenheit scale and seen it was minus four—which converts to minus twenty Celsius!

We laughed and laughed. I no longer felt quite so soft.

I have thought about that experience quite a bit over the last few days.

When I stepped outside that morning, my body was telling me, from years of experience, that it was cold outside. I was completely in agreement with that information until Grace reported that it was minus four. I took a round out of my body because I was sure that the data had to be right and what my body was telling me had to be wrong. "Minus four is minus four," I told my body, "and you are being ridiculous." I don't think I would have gone out on the snowmobile if I had known that it was minus twenty. But the data said minus four, and I was confident I had nothing to fear at that temperature—my mind was quite certain about that, regardless of what my body was trying to tell me.

I had lived on the Canadian prairies for twenty-five years, almost half of my life. I know what cold is, and yet I did not trust my experience and inner knowledge. I didn't even question the information that I was being given. I completely accepted it and lived according to it, instead of paying attention to what my years of experience and my hurting body parts were trying to tell me.

That sobered me quite a bit. It was a good lesson for me as I continue to navigate my way in this age of digital information. Perhaps it is a reminder that I should listen more attentively to my experience and the understanding I have gathered over my years on this planet. Surely I should not be so quick to relegate my accumulated wisdom to the archives as useless information. After all, in this case, it would have saved me from the pain of some pretty tender ears over the next few hours.

I believe that God has placed in us an awareness of His presence (Romans 1:18-22). But I also believe that I can make choices in my life that cloud that awareness to the point where I do not listen to it and respond to other voices. I must practice listening to the voice of love, testing what I hear in order to be sure that it is a voice that can be trusted. When something doesn't make sense, I must go back and check the thermometer. By following God's voice, I will be spared from the greatest hurt of all—a sense of separation from Him.

Morning

*"For we live by believing and not
by seeing." – 2 Corinthians 5:7*

The anticipation of my first cup of coffee usually goes a long way to getting me up every morning. In fact, it can be a problem. When I awaken a little too early, I have to convince myself to catch a little more sleep in spite of the lure of that first sip of morning coffee.

A few days ago, the start to my day was normal. I made my coffee and savored my first sip. Then I decided to go into the Convivios Room in our home, put on some worship music, stand by the large east-facing windows, and watch the sunrise. We have had many beautiful sunrises over the years, and it looked like this morning would provide another one. Like a good cup of morning coffee, I never get tired of sunrises. I love the morning sun and the anticipation of its arrival. A few scattered clouds above the eastern horizon promised to provide quite a show as the radiance of the sun awakened the drab clouds with the brilliance of dawn.

I generally start each day consciously recognizing God's love and provision. This morning was no different as I stood there in silence, cup in hand, mindful of the words of the music that was playing. I wished for a moment that God would be present in a tangible and physical form. I wished that many people I knew could get just one hug from Him in person, one comforting touch in the midst of their sorrow, one hug that they would never forget, one gaze demonstrating His unfathomable love for them. Surely that would change the world for them.

I wonder if, from time to time, most of us have a little trouble letting love in. Sometimes I think I even block it out, barricaded

inside my preoccupied subconscious mind. Maybe a part of me wants to believe that I don't really need love and that if I did, it would be a sign of weakness and dependency. No doubt that is a form of pride—and pride leaves us losers in the end, lost in a wilderness of self-deception.

If God appeared beside me today and I was given one loving glance from Him in person, surely I would no longer doubt His love. Surely then I would realize how loved we all are. Surely then I would be able to live in hope.

As I stood there and listened to the Spirit, I noticed a jet trail tracing across the morning sky towards the east. The plane was likely at 20,000 or 30,000 feet, allowing the vapor trail to reflect the rising sun before the clouds could be painted. It was a brilliant pink/orange line growing ever longer. Try as I might, I could not see the jet that was obviously present and leaving the glowing trail across the sky. Yet it had to be there—I knew that because the evidence of its presence was unmistakable.

A smile formed, and tears were close, as a feeling of tenderness took over—a gift, a deep tenderness, reassuring me of unfathomable love. I could not see, but I could believe.

Lost Keys

"And when he has found it, he will joyfully carry it home on his shoulders. When he arrives, he will call together his friends and neighbors, saying, 'Rejoice with me because I have found my lost sheep.' In the same way, there is more joy in heaven over one lost sinner who repents and returns to God than over ninety-nine others who are righteous and haven't strayed away!" – Luke 15:5-7

It was a dark winter evening. Grace brought me to the car dealership to pick up my old Toyota truck, where a person, who had used it for a few weeks, had left it earlier in the day. I grabbed the door handle, hoping to jump in, return home, and carry on with my evening, allowing Grace to continue on her way to her meeting. The door was locked—which was not at all what I had expected.

I called the person who had borrowed my truck to ask where the keys were. The response was disappointing: "I left them in the truck and by mistake locked the door." Oh, well. Fortunately, Grace was still there. We decided to go home, retrieve the second key, and return so that I could get my truck off the lot before it was closed for the night.

It was not so easily done. Back home, I went to retrieve the keys from the location where we stored all current keys, but there was no key for the Toyota. I normally keep close tabs on the various vehicle keys and have a spare readily accessible. Grace was still hoping to get to her meeting—she was now at least half an hour late—so I hurriedly went through my dresser drawers upstairs. I found a set of unlabeled keys and in a rush assumed—contrary to what my subconscious was telling me—that they were the right ones.

Off we went, with keys in hand, to the lot, which was still open. In the darkness, I fumbled with the locked truck handle. My "present self" was surprised. My "wiser self" said: "I told you so." I looked at the keys, which were clearly labeled "Yamaha." I laughed out loud, feeling like an idiot. I have never had a Yamaha truck—a Yamaha Rhino off-road vehicle and a Yamaha motorcycle, yes, but not a Yamaha truck.

Grace was still patiently waiting for me. I apologized, and back we went to our home. Each trip was at least ten minutes one way, and this was now our fifth trip, not counting the time we had spent looking for the lost keys. Grace had graciously given up on her meeting.

Back at home, the search for the missing key intensified. I removed dresser drawers, dumping the contents in a pile on my bed. Ridiculous stuff had accumulated in those drawers. I sifted and sorted, having no luck whatsoever with finding the spare key. There was now no chance of retrieving the truck that evening, but I continued my quest. I retraced and re-examined possible previous trips, trying to think when I had last had the other key. I even phoned our son Ryan, from whom I had purchased the truck years ago, to see if he still had a key—which was ridiculous, as he lives four hours away. I was very angry with myself because I knew there was a second key.

I returned to the original location where the key should have been stored, examining every crack and corner. All of a sudden, it came to me. I had given that person the spare key when I had handed over the truck. I had no idea why I had done that, other than that it was during a very busy time in the middle of the Christmas season. The "regular" key was under the floor mat of the truck, where I always kept it for easy access. After all, it was our "farm truck," as we called it.

I now knew that both keys were securely locked in the truck. We have a British Columbia Automobile Association membership, so that would be an option in the morning—but the schedule for the morning was intense, and the prospect of waiting for BCAA was not comforting. I wondered if the dealership, where the truck was parked, would have a "slim jim" used to break into locked vehicles.

Looking for lost things can be all-encompassing, going way beyond what is rational in many cases. When Grace is looking for things, the search can continue for days, as she relentlessly tries to recover what has been the lost.

I remember some fearful times when we thought we had "lost" one or more of our children. That was horrifying. Fortunately, we always found them, but the feeling of having lost one was overwhelming. It seemed that nothing else mattered compared to finding the lost one.

As I think about how lost stuff can haunt me until it is found, I can't help but think of Jesus' three parables recorded in Luke 15. Each of the three stories—apparently told in succession to the same audience, Pharisees and teachers of religious law—is intended to communicate how God will pursue the lost.

The first story concerns a man who loses one sheep out of his herd of one hundred. What does he do? He goes in search of the one that is lost. When it is found, he joyfully carries it home on his shoulders and then throws a party, saying, "Rejoice with me because I have found my lost sheep" (Luke 15:3-7).

In the second parable, a woman loses one of ten coins, and she turns over everything in her home until she finds it. (This sounds like Grace.) And when she finds it, she throws a party and tells her friends and neighbors, "Rejoice with me because I have found my lost coin" (Luke 15:8-10).

The third, one of the most profound parables that Jesus told, is the story of the prodigal son (Luke 15:11-32). Apparently, the father allows his son to leave with his inheritance, knowing full well that it will be squandered. But then he watches in anticipation every day, never losing hope that his son will be "found." And when he sees his son coming from a long distance off, he runs to him, filled with love and compassion. And he throws a party to celebrate, saying, "He was lost, but now he is found."

All three of these parables emphasize looking for the lost. From these parables, it would appear that God is persistently looking for us, longing to embrace us and throw a party when we are found.

It is unfathomable, really, that God is looking for the lost and apparently not willing to give up. That is good news!

When I was a child, I remember being told that if I ever felt lost, I should just stay where I was and trust that the people who loved me would find me—resisting the temptation to panic and run, hoping to find a safe place. Maybe we try a little too hard to figure this all out. Maybe we need to sit still for a bit and realize that running may not be the best way to be found. Maybe we need to simply trust that the One who loves us beyond imagination will find us and will safely carry us home.

The next morning, Grace took me back to the car dealership. I inquired if there was a person around who knew how to break into locked vehicles. I was told yes, there was, and he would be with me shortly. A few minutes later, a fellow showed up with a specialized tool, and I soon had my keys. Looking at him, I almost asked where he had learned that skill. I chose instead to just say thank you and go on my way.

Cloud Watching

"Who can understand the spreading
of the clouds?" – Job 36:29

It was a quiet Sunday at our home in British Columbia's Lower Fraser Valley. God had spread a blanket of snow, like a down quilt, over the fields, adding to the beauty visible in every direction. The snow, about six inches of it, had fallen twenty-four hours earlier and had since nestled into the land, adding texture to the flat surface of the day before. On this day, I was drawn over and over again to observe the beauty. A predominantly blue sky, a rarity here at this time of year, added to the magical sight. There was little, if any, wind, but movement aloft and the passing of the day continually produced new and magnificent pictures all around us.

The usual cloud pattern around here in the winter is stratiform—huge layers of clouds that block out the sky for days. Individual clouds are lost in the jumble of a sky overpopulated with them. Today was different. Clouds formed and dissipated ever so gently. These were convective clouds, formed by rising water vapor in the area. Those droplets of water clumped together, forming various shapes, and then disconnected and disappeared.

The clouds of today reminded me of the ones we often see in the Cariboo region of B.C.'s interior—and the kind I used to watch with my grandfather when I was growing up on the Canadian prairies. We would lie on the grass of his farmyard and identify shapes, often animals, that morphed into something else quite quickly.

"Look over there—a horse just like King," he would say. King was the name of the horse that was used for various tasks around the farm even though the farm had a tractor. I can almost hear his

voice as he pointed his ancient finger to a formation. It struck me today that he was then at the age that I am at now. Perhaps my grandchildren think my fingers look ancient too.

At lunch, over a great bowl of Grace's homemade soup, thick with ham and vegetables of every kind, I once again found myself watching a cloud in the east. It surrounded a patch of blue, leaving a window, an aperture, that some unseen hand slowly closed until no light could get through.

This led to a conversation with Grace about how a cloud can appear to be a solid barrier to an unknowing observer. If all we had previously experienced was clear sky, we would likely be frightened at the prospect of flying a plane into a wall of cloud. I admit that flying into clouds has always felt strange to me, especially when the plane trembled as the cloud swallowed it up.

Grace and I wondered how birds fly in clouds, or fog for that matter. A little research on the Internet provided all kinds of theories, including one that they don't fly in clouds in most cases because they have been known to crash into things! I guess we will leave that with God for now.

I believe that God uses everything in creation to communicate to us. Nature has been one of my best teachers, and so it was on this occasion. Life presents us with many "clouds"—challenges that appear to be impenetrable barriers. The really frightening ones loom big on the horizon, consuming the peace that God gives. I have encountered many such clouds in my life and believe that I am learning that there is almost always a path through. Oddly, when I look back, that "cloud" often has disappeared.

Transition and Trees

"If you cling to your life, you will lose it; but if you give up your life for me, you will find it." – Matthew 10:39

"Spend the afternoon. You can't take it with you."
– Annie Dillard

It has not been a harsh winter here in the Fraser Valley—unlike most of the rest of North America, where record snowfalls have been the norm. Many of us in the Fraser Valley are probably bracing ourselves for a final winter blast, feeling guilty, as if we are to blame for the thrashing that La Nina has given the rest of the continent over the last few months. Perhaps, if we just keep quiet and duck, La Nina will not notice us, and we will make it through to spring without too much damage. It is early February, and the pussy willows on our neighbor's tree are already out.

Nevertheless, winter has taken its toll in the forest near our home. Some old trees, weakened by their years, have been snapped off halfway up their trunks, exposing their hearts to the elements and the many invasive pests that abound in the forest. This is often a death sentence for the tree. The seed-bearing branches are generally the ones located higher up the trunk, and they now have been snapped off, never to bear again. For a tree, this is aging in place. It cannot seek shelter. It has no choice but to remain where it sprang to life many years ago and allow the elements to have their way. When it was a vibrant tree, it could bend much more easily to a wind, shedding the wind's full force. Today, its branches are brittle. On some branches, the bark has fallen away, leaving huge scars. When the tree was young, a branch broken off could easily be replaced. In fact, natural pruning like this often seems to invigorate a tree. But not so any more. This is how it ends. The tree will slowly rot away, or a strong wind will push the remaining trunk over and pull the life-giving roots out of the ground, ending its life.

Like those trees, I am in a transition stage of life. I am almost sixty. I feel that there is still a lot of life left in me, but I am also aware of changes that are necessary, changes that I must accept— no, that I must embrace.

Grace's Dad died a year ago today. In order to remember him, she sent a beautiful short e-mail out to all of us, his children by birth or marriage. A picture accompanied it. It was a picture of her Mom and Dad, perhaps not yet twenty years old, standing between their parents. Grace's Dad's parents were on his right and her Mom's parents on her left. They were in the middle, looking straight ahead, smiles on their faces, holding hands. Grace's Mom's Dad was looking over at his daughter—I wonder what he was thinking.

Grace's words and that photo have stuck with me today. Are Grace and I now at the time of our lives where we must willingly stand on the side, with the next generation in the middle? Is it now our role to do what we can, as the years take their toll, to support, protect, and nurture the future generations coming along? I suppose we could resist that development and insist that we "stay in the middle"; after all, we may still have many dreams and hopes.

Then I think about the trees in the forest. They have to accept their role and support the new growth. They can still provide shade and stabilize the earth with their roots. Perhaps the young trees growing beside them will eventually take more of the nutrients and water from the soil they share and unintentionally weaken the old trees, but that is what happens. Those young trees represent the life of the old trees—that is how the old trees will live on. As their ancient bark sloughs away, allowing woodpeckers to feast on their flesh, the birds will leave the young trees alone, giving the young trees time to become strong enough to resist those pounding beaks at a later date.

In time, the old trees will finally fall to the ground, become covered by moss, and turn to humus. As the old trees slip away, their passing opens the way for new life. To live well and then give life away for others—is that not a life worth living? I think that is what Jesus tried to teach us. After all, we must pass away from this earth in order to reach our heavenly home.

I like Annie Dillard's advice about spending our afternoons. As long as I have an "afternoon," I pray that I will reach my branches towards the sky in gratitude and reach those same branches out to love those growing up in the earth around me. I hope, too, that when it is time for me to leave, my life will enrich the ground from which the next generation will grow. What greater life can there be than to provide a good place for others to grow?

Tree Sap and Suffering

"God blesses those who mourn, for they
will be comforted." – Matthew 5:4

"From now on, don't let anyone trouble me with
these things. For I bear on my body the scars
that show I belong to Jesus." – Galatians 6:17

A Tuesday morning in the Cariboo. I lifted my head from my pillow and looked down the creek through the uncurtained window. I do this every morning when I awaken, hoping and half expecting to see something of interest. This morning, I was rewarded. A "dog" was walking down the middle of the creek, which was a perfect frozen pathway at this time of year. At first, I wondered if it was a wolf. I decided to awaken Grace because this could be a sight she wouldn't want to miss. We lay there transfixed. As we watched, we soon realized that the "dog" was a red fox—a very healthy one, who pranced right up to our front yard and then ran off into the forest, his red color magnified by the white snow. He looked as if he was strutting his stuff, and he had every reason to do so. His appearance was a great treat to start the day.

I got up and walked over to the window to look in the other direction, hoping to catch a glimpse of the fox crossing our meadow. To my surprise, there was something on our driveway. Morning vision caused me to announce that there was a tractor on our driveway. Further inspection, and a little clearing of my senses, showed me I had been wrong. It was actually a fallen tree. The winds overnight had dropped an eighty-foot spruce across our driveway.

I called our son Ryan, requesting that he bring his largest chainsaw when he came later in the morning. We had an old Homelite chainsaw that my Dad had given me, but I wasn't sure how well it would work.

I pulled out the old saw—heavy in comparison to today's models—and thought of my Dad. When he bought this saw, he was likely younger than I am today. Now, it was with me in the Cariboo, a place where my Dad loves to be as well. I fueled and oiled it and gave it a pull. It turned over with no problem and, within five or six more pulls, roared to life. I remembered trying to sharpen the blade sometime earlier and knew that, at best, it would cut in a curved fashion if used on a log of any size. The tree lying across our driveway would certainly fit into that category. I figured I could at least limb it, and then we could finish it off when Ryan arrived.

Well, the saw worked great, and by the time Ryan arrived, there were only a couple of cuts remaining. With Grace's help, it didn't take us long until everything was cleaned up, with only a huge pile of branches left as a memorial to the tree's existence.

I wrote about that tree earlier. The previous summer, woodpeckers had started working on it and had burrowed deeply into its trunk. The top of the tree looked healthy, full of branches and pinecones, but the hole in the trunk determined its future. This morning, it lay across our driveway, its life as a tree over.

As is so often the case out here, if I take time to listen, there is a lesson to be learned about my own life. This is what I learned as I pondered this fallen spruce throughout the day.

When the tree had snapped off during the night, we had heard nothing. It had fallen to its death unnoticed by us just a hundred meters away. The tree had broken off where the woodpeckers had hammered away, causing the gaping wound that I had noticed the previous summer. The woodpeckers were after bugs that had eaten the heart out of the tree at this level of the trunk. I imagine that some form of wound must have initiated this process. Wounds to trees are not uncommon. Perhaps in this case it was a bump from the lawn mower. A windstorm or heavy snowfall can also snap off a branch, leaving exposed wood. But usually a tree's sap coats such wounds to prevent infestation by bugs and disease. If the sap flows freely, the tree will live on. For some reason, this time the tree was unable to protect itself. The tree was unable to seal off the wound with its blood. Perhaps the sap did not flow freely enough.

My thoughts turned to loss in our human lives. We don't seem to get very old before we start to experience loss and the associated pain. I wonder if we do harm by not allowing ourselves to "bleed." We may be tempted to deny the loss, deny the pain, distract ourselves from the hurt. But if we do that, we may prevent our "sap" from flowing and deprive ourselves of protection and healing. Yes, a scar may form, but if we do not allow ourselves to bleed, to hurt, that may leave us exposed to greater harm and suffering. Open wounds can allow an enemy to invade and infect our hearts. It is difficult for us to suffer, and equally as hard to watch those we love suffer, but maybe our attempts to prevent suffering can actually cause harm. Perhaps the suffering protects the wound from being a gateway for more harmful infections.

I continue to believe that God has built loving systems into His creation that can teach us how to live. Perhaps suffering is a gift to help us heal and move ahead in our lives while we are finding our way home. Not one of us will get home without scars, and it may well be the scars that bring us safely there in the end.

Funds for Philishave

*"Look at the birds. They don't plant or harvest
or store food in barns, for your heavenly Father
feeds them. And aren't you far more valuable
to him than they are?" – Matthew 6:26*

I filled up the bird feeder yesterday. It was an "awful" day—maybe not in comparison to the day they had farther north in Kitimat, B.C., where over five feet of snow fell in a little more than twenty-four hours—but a dark, wet day nevertheless. On such days, several types of birds hide out in the cedar hedge beside our home, hunkering down against the elements. Giving them an opportunity for a free meal close to their temporary haven seemed like a good thing to do. They were soon darting out and helping themselves to some seeds before flying back to shelter. They had to take a risk and come out of their comfort zone to enjoy the plentiful food that Grace and I had provided. I guess we could have hung the feeder in the trees, but then we wouldn't have been able to see the birds in their God-given beauty.

The bird feeder had been more or less empty for a few days. The birds can find other food, but it felt good to give them an ample supply in their time of need in the middle of winter. Maybe being able to give them a treat on a day like today blesses us as much as it does them.

I got to thinking about how God has provided for us over the years. I could tell many stories about this. Maybe I need to write them down before they are lost.

As I look back on my life, I think I have wasted far too much time and energy worrying about stuff. I can say that now—as hindsight is generally 20/20—but at the time we frequently faced seemingly insurmountable challenges, often related to paying bills. Maybe the worry helped us get to this point of our life as well, but I wonder if there is a difference between being worried and being concerned—the latter maybe being more healthy and something that had to be learned over time. Worry costs us life. Concern can be a great teacher that draws the past, the present, hope, and trust together. I think I worried too much.

This story happened when Grace and I were living in Calgary while I attended university. To say the least, we did not have much money. We still often joke about the time we ate bologna every day for a week. We were never without food, but the choices were often limited. But, as I look back, I see those as good days.

During that time, we were serving as youth sponsors in our church. Of course, in a city as big as Calgary, it could require quite a bit of driving just to get to the church, and even more if we had to use our vehicle to transport the kids from the church to an event. I remember clearly one Friday night. We had put the weekly five dollars' worth of gas into our car and headed off to the church, with no intention of driving any further than that. When we arrived, we found out that the intended transportation had not shown up. We were asked if we would be willing to fill in. Having learned to be polite, we agreed—but inside I was not in agreement at all!

I remember telling God that I loved Him dearly but that this was ridiculous. We hardly had enough funds to provide transportation for our little family, and we most certainly did not have enough to be shuttling youth around that night. To top it off, it was a progressive supper, requiring multiple destinations, as we went from home to home to be served each menu item. This would require a lot of fuel. I told God with respect (I hope)—after all, who am I to tell God anything?—that this was His problem and that He needed to pay us back ten to one for the gas that we had put into our car. (I could probably have used a reminder that the car was actually His and not mine to begin with.) I can't believe that I did that, but I was tired and stressed. I had obviously forgotten that God was the Creator of the universe and everything in it and He could handle this too. But I had to bark out my demand for repayment from

Him. If He required ten percent of everything we made in the form of a tithe, then in this case perhaps He could provide ten times as much in return. I can't believe that I didn't get struck by lightning. I surely deserved it.

The next day, a Saturday, we went over to my parents' home, maybe to get a meal. They lived close by.

When we arrived, Dad was cleaning out the garage. It was full of the stuff that accumulates, all by itself, in a typical garage. Over the years, Dad had attended various auctions where he would buy stuff in the hope of reselling it to make a bit of extra money. As I walked by a garbage can, I peered inside and noticed a bunch of boxes labeled "Philishave." I knew that was a razor company. I pulled one of the boxes out of the can and opened it. Inside were brand new rotary shaver heads, still in individual boxes for retail sale. As I recall, there were two and half boxes in the garbage can. I asked Dad if I could have them. He said, "Yes, of course. Either by you or by the garbage can, they are leaving my home."

I went into their home and took out the phone book, checking the yellow pages for razor repairs. I found a company in downtown Calgary that seemed like a possible market. I phoned, and to my surprise they offered to buy them all from me for seventy-five dollars! Grace and I were shocked. My thoughts turned back to my conversation with God from the night before. He had repaid us fifteen fold! I delivered the razors downtown right away and got my seventy-five dollars before the company owners could change their minds. We were humbled and blessed.

I need to keep remembering such stories. God has been with us throughout all of our lives. Yes, at times, we have wondered how we were going to get through, and those are good times to remember stories like this.

Don't get me wrong. I am not advocating bargaining with God. But this story is evidence of His unfathomable love for me, even when I am cranky. God has told us in Matthew 6:26 that we are "far more valuable" than birds. And we are.

Unconditional Love and Unconditional Approval

"Jesus traveled through all the towns and villages of that area, teaching in the synagogues and announcing the Good News about the Kingdom. And he healed every kind of disease and illness. When he saw the crowds, he had compassion on them because they were confused and helpless, like sheep without a shepherd. He said to his disciples, 'The harvest is great, but the workers are few. So pray to the Lord who is in charge of the harvest; ask him to send more workers into his fields.'" – Matthew 9:35-38

My thoughts were turned to the concepts of love and approval this morning as I read a perplexing few verses in Matthew (9:35-38). I am still curious about why Jesus encouraged His disciples to pray to the Lord of the harvest (assuming that that is God) to send out more workers because the harvest was great. Would the Lord of the harvest not be aware of the condition of the harvest? The passage also records that He said this to His disciples—but conspicuously absent was a directive that they should go out and be the workers in the fields themselves. I almost felt irreverent as I tried to understand. After a while, I decided to leave the matter to perk for a bit.

Then my thoughts turned to the early verses of this passage. Jesus was traveling from town to town, teaching in the synagogues—not only announcing the Good News but healing "every kind of disease and illness" (Matthew 9:35). Then the passage says: "When he saw the crowds, he had compassion on them because they were confused and helpless, like sheep without a shepherd" (Matthew 9: 36). There had to have been religious leaders and Pharisees in those crowds. Yet, the text clearly states that when He saw the crowds, Jesus had compassion on them. By now, many within the religious community saw Him as an enemy, and they made no bones about it. They had been present for many of the miracles, but this had only perplexed and angered them, driving them to the point that they were unwilling to see.

Jesus loved the crowds—He did not approve of their actions, but He loved them. God's love for us is unconditional love. "Can anything ever separate us from Christ's love?" the apostle Paul asked. And then he answered: "I am convinced that nothing can ever separate us from God's love....Nothing in all creation will ever be able to separate us from the love of God that is revealed in Christ Jesus our Lord" (Romans 8:35, 38, 39). The beautiful story of the prodigal son was told by Jesus to a group of Pharisees for sure, in a crowd that perhaps also included tax collectors and other sinners. This story, told in Luke 15, emphasizes what unconditional love is. Unconditional love simply is. It is a state of being that cannot change. Perhaps this is the strongest characteristic of all creation— that God is love (1 John 4:8). And from that point we carry on. It is the foundation of all.

Somewhere along the line, perhaps in the Garden of Eden, the concept of approval raised its head. Human beings sinned, lost God's approval, and were banished to live a miserable existence until all will be reunited in Him at just the right time (Ephesians 1:9-11). All creation joined in the fall and was left abandoned to itself. So, we struggle for approval, hoping that in gaining approval we will once again be restored to love.

As a parent, I am quite certain that I did harm to our children by adding to the confusion between approval and love, perhaps because I did not even understand the difference myself. My children constantly heard the message: "If I approve of your action, then you are loved. If I do not approve of your action, you are not loved." And this is the way we lived. I am constantly drawn to win approval from others because then I think I will feel loved. But, at the end of the day, I am not loved—I am approved, but that approval can be withdrawn at any time. That approval also likely has as much to do with my own state of mind or sense of security as anything else. I give approval and withdraw it. I receive approval and lose it. I live bewildered at times because I have no idea how to earn that approval or how I lost it in the first place. I move from person to person, group to group, seeking approval, hoping to feel loved. It seems to work from time to time, but then it vanishes, and I am left feeling unloved once again, only to repeat the cycle over and over.

Solace for me often comes in solitude or quietness. I love being "out in the bush"—and oddly, that is where I seem to be most aware of being loved. Of course, there are also other times, when I feel loved in the clutter of normal city living, but seldom do I spend significant time outside that I do not feel loved. I did not gain the approval of the trees, the birds, and the blades of grass, and yet I feel loved in the bush.

And that is the difference! God loves us unconditionally. It is a state of being—me standing there with nothing but what He miraculously created me to be, and in that place I am unconditionally loved. He disapproves of my actions, and I deserve that disapproval, but that does not change His love. There is a huge difference between approval and love. The former, approval, can lead me to a neurotic life; the latter leaves me with a sense of security and even belonging. And that is Good News!

"Then Christ will make his home in your hearts as you trust in him. Your roots will grow down into God's love and keep you strong. And may you have the power to understand, as all God's people should, how wide, how long, and how deep his love is. May you experience the love of Christ, though it is too great to understand fully. Then you will be made complete with all the fullness of life and power that comes from God" (Ephesians 3:17-19).

Loved

"I knew you before I formed you
in your mother's womb.
Before you were born I set you apart
and appointed you as my prophet
to the nations."– Jeremiah 1:5

It was Friday night, at the end of a very intense and challenging week. I was very tired; maybe "weary" would be a better word to describe how I felt. It was not as if I was dissatisfied with the way most of the challenges of the week had seemed to sort themselves out—but I still felt a deep exhaustion.

There was great reason for delight, as our newest grandchild had just made it home on Thursday after five days in neonatal intensive care. Adam Hunter had started his life in ICU, as had our other grandson, Ethan, seven years earlier. One's mind can slip into the muck of despair so easily when such innocence needs to be rescued from imminent danger. I am grateful for God's hand and for those whom He equipped to restore both of our grandsons to health.

As we lay in bed, both Grace and I had our laptops, and for some reason we found ourselves looking at photos of our family, especially our grandchildren. In moments, my troubled spirit was at peace. It was very noticeable. We reminisced as picture after picture triggered a memory. We laughed together as we saw the animation on the faces and, on occasion, the somewhat reflective expressions. Even as I write this, a smile effortlessly crosses my face as I picture each one of our four grandchildren, Asia, Ethan, Myra, and Adam, beautiful gifts beyond description. I am quite certain that they cannot appreciate what they mean to us, that they give us something that we cannot give ourselves. When they entered this world, they immediately found a place in our hearts, shaped by them and only available to them, a tender place where they will continue to reside.

There are many that reside in tender places in my heart. Thinking of each one brings joy. Depending on their situation, concern or even sadness may be close at hand, but the joy is still there too. I can safely say that we take delight in our grandchildren and our children, and many other beloved people too.

These thoughts reminded me of a Bible verse: "For the LORD your God is living among you. He is a mighty savior. He will take delight in you with gladness. With his love, he will calm all your fears. He will rejoice over you with joyful songs" (Zephaniah 3:17). How incomprehensible is that? And yet, how comprehensible is the great joy a little child, only moments old, can give? Newborn babies have not achieved anything at all. They just showed up, and we were immediately in love. And to think that God knew us even earlier than that: "I knew you before I formed you in your mother's womb" (Jeremiah 1:5). As inexplicable as it may seem, we just showed up, and God loved us. We can do nothing to increase or decrease His love for us. In this moment, we are loved as a newborn child entering this world, innocent and touched by God's grace.

The Flowers of the Winter Olympics

*"The LORD says, 'I will guide you along the
best pathway for your life. I will advise you
and watch over you.'...Unfailing love surrounds
those who trust the LORD." – Psalm 32:8, 10*

*"The flowers of late winter and early spring
occupy places in our hearts
well out of proportion to their size."
– Gertrude S. Wister*

As I write this, it is February 24, 2010, and there is still officially a month left of winter. The Winter Olympics are still going on in nearby Vancouver. And yet, as I look out my window, I see magnolias offering up their beautiful pink petals, a harbinger of spring. I see brilliant yellow forsythias denying the darkness of a rainy morning. I see daffodils, their trumpet-shaped heads twisting, trying to find the morning sun. I see cherry blossoms multiplying along the streets. These are but a few of the flowers that have awoken to a very early spring. They obviously did not check their calendars to see if this was the right time to take the risk and blossom. In fact, they could not resist. I am certain that, for many of these plants, this is the earliest they have blossomed in decades. They know that the risk of frost still exists, don't they? And yet, there they are—and not just a few of them either. The 2010 Winter Olympics welcomed guests to Vancouver, not with snow, but with flowers!

Our personal lives have been inundated with challenge after challenge over the last few months. If I step back and try to put our lives into perspective, I realize the challenges have been minor compared to the challenges some others have had to face, but for me the journey of late has been quite arduous. If life consists of hilltops and valleys, then recently they have been squashed together, at times seeming to overlap. How can one live on a mountaintop and in a valley at the same time? But this is our life right now—the sudden loss of a parent, the engagement of a son, and much more. How can I absorb all of these things happening at once? Perhaps I cannot, and in that admission may lie an answer of sorts. If absorbing means understanding and having the time to plan a proper response, then that may be impossible.

So how then do I live? Do I rely on what is inside me as my compass? Do I trust what has been imprinted in me and believe that it will guide me? Can I live at peace and just carry on, believing that all will be well at some point?

I have shed tears of sorrow and tears of joy within minutes of each other, expressing emotions apparently on opposite ends of a spectrum. But perhaps that spectrum is circular, and the two extremes meet at a place that engages my heart and soul. I cannot seem to control my responses to events—does that mean that I can trust my responses to be right?

Once again, I look out the window at the flowers. They are abundant, even though the calendar would have warned them to stay hidden a little longer for their own good. They could not stop themselves from blooming. Circumstances and their inherent nature made them bloom—it was what was in them to do. It may be to their peril, but events happened to awaken them, and this is how they had to respond.

Is that similar to our own lives? We strive to have some degree of control and order, but there is little we can do to prevent the sudden incursion of crisis and chaos. Do such times unavoidably produce a more basic human response, whether for good or ill? I fear that our chaotic times will rob us of the inner strength needed to respond in good ways. I believe that we need time to reflect, meditate, and pray in order to exercise our inner strength properly. Yet, we seem to be preoccupied and distracted by so much else, leaving little time for the incubation of our souls.

I am grateful for the many who have offered up prayers to support us through our chaotic times. Indeed, we have felt the prayers like the wind beneath our wings. But, even more, I am grateful for the voice that speaks gently to me in the stillness of the chaos, telling me that I am loved. That love is not contingent on how put-together I may feel or on how put-together I present myself. I do not have to perform acceptably to be loved. I am loved all along the pathway of my life, no matter how crazy that pathway seems to be from time to time.

Pressing On

*"Even when I walk through
the darkest valley,
I will not be afraid,
for you are close beside me.
Your rod and your staff
comfort me." – Psalm 23:4*

The deluge of seasonal rain has reluctantly given way to sunshine, and we are thoroughly enjoying it. This morning, I rose early and waited for the sun to rise above the mountains in the east. New blossoms welcomed the warm sun, as they exploded into color.

As it began to get light, we headed out on our morning walk on the familiar trail that we use almost every day—familiar and yet dynamic, as there is always change if we are willing to pay attention. Yesterday we noticed the first trilliums of the year.

As we rounded a corner, it appeared that a "wall" closed off the trail ahead. Having gone this way many times before, we knew better, but a first-time traveler might have looked for an alternate route, assuming that the trail must come to a dead end. The "wall" was only a bush darkened by the early morning shadows, with the trail veering off to the right through a beautiful forest.

I commented to Grace: "Look. The trail is closed ahead."

Understandably, she questioned what I was saying, because we had walked past that place hundreds of times over the years.

"But doesn't it look closed?"

We talked about how in life we are often confronted with "blocked pathways," barriers that can keep us from progressing along our journey. They may tempt us to take an alternate route, assuming that we cannot possibly get through the situation in front of us. Over the years, we have learned that, just like on the trail, it is often necessary to press on towards the barrier and trust that there will be a way through somehow. Looking back, we can almost chuckle as we remember the fear that gripped us as we approached one of those barriers, only to see the path leading through become visible.

I suppose that this is a lesson that we all have to learn on our own—and keep learning. In time, we might even learn to see that the unknown ahead of us is more of an adventure to be embraced than a wall to be avoided.

Of course, there are some unknowns that we cannot avoid and that do lead to barriers—but perhaps they, too, can be adventures of a sort.

Into the Wind

"The LORD...never grows weak or weary...
He gives power to the weak
and strength to the powerless.
Even youths will become weak and tired,
and young men will fall in exhaustion.
But those who trust in the LORD
will find new strength.
They will soar high on wings like eagles.
They will run and not grow weary.
They will walk and not faint."
– Isaiah 40:28-31

"With my God I can scale any wall."
– Psalm 18:29

Relentless! That was the only way to describe it. The wind had howled for hours through the night, and there was no sign of it letting up. Plastic chairs had scurried for cover on our deck, tangling their legs around the railings to keep from being blown off the property. Metal chairs on the lower patio had been lifted and transported out into our yard, along with the accompanying glass table. Our swing had been moved several feet from its perceived place of safety up against a wall. Branches littered the yard. Peak wind speeds had inched close to a fifty-year-old record, hitting ninety-five kilometers per hour. At our altitude, just 250 feet above sea level, the dense air moving at that speed can do a lot of damage. At the peak, over 110,000 homes were without power. Fortunately, we were not one of them—this time.

We decided to venture out to experience the intensity and power of the storm. I have always felt a strange compulsion to "feel" a storm like that firsthand. Grace was game, as was our dog Coco, so off we went, alert to the danger of flying debris. The roar coming from the bush behind our place was eerie. Explosions broke the monotonous roar of the wind as tree after tree gave way.

To our surprise, in spite of the wind, we noticed a bald eagle soaring maybe 150 to 200 feet above the ground, facing into the wind. We were transfixed, caught in what seemed a sacred moment, as we watched this eagle. It seemed virtually unaffected by the wind, almost stationary, hanging like a kite on a string. It looked as if it was actually at peace in the relentless wind that was storming through the forest, felling trees and stripping branches. The slightest movement seemed to allow the eagle to progress forward into the wind. It had deliberately chosen not to flee from the wind, but to defy its power, even though it was as light as a feather in comparison to the heavy objects that were tumbling in retreat before this wind. In spite of the conditions, we remained on the path for some time, watching this wonder. We were amazed that the eagle had chosen to be in that wind, facing that relentless gale, rather than seeking shelter.

I expect this event will stay in my mind for a long time. Life seems so full of sorrow, challenge, and adversity, causing us to forget the promise that God's unfathomable love will be with us in any circumstances. The possibility that we can choose to face the winds of sadness, sorrow, adversity, and violence, knowing that we will be held lovingly in that place, is great news. Knowing this, we can choose to live in trust and be at peace.

Spring Cold

"I will never fail you.
I will never abandon you."
– Hebrews 13:5

"For I can do everything through Christ,
who gives me strength."
– Philippians 4:13

"If you are going through hell, keep going."
– Winston Churchill.

It was sunny outside, trees were blossoming, and the temperature was rising. Inside, I was getting my rest and feeling secure, having been vaccinated with the latest flu shot mandated by the local health authority. But it is not that easy to isolate myself from exposure in this world where we increasingly share the same space. If I were a flu virus, I would wait behind a tree until the health authority had decided which one of us it was going to target this year and then decide if this was my year to attack or not. In fact, the way it appears to be working, the vaccine may actually compromise the general population's defenses and increase the spread of infection.

All right, that may be overstated. I am an advocate of well-researched vaccines and grateful for the incredible impact they have had on diseases the world over. What I have trouble accepting is the mandating of vaccines such as the annual flu shot when the health authorities have such a poor track record in predicting which strain of flu virus will appear in a given year. I wonder if some day we will look back on this with some regret for not being more careful in what we make mandatory.

Okay, I'm ranting, but I have good reason. I have what some have called the "spring cold." I have watched as it has bounced around our community for a while and managed to stay out of its way—until a few days ago. I felt it move in at a meeting last week and hoped my security forces—my white blood cells—would notice the intruder and target it for elimination. A couple of days later, I realized the battle was lost. Surrender had now become the only option. After three more days, I was done. Of course, some rest in the prior few days might have given my security forces a better chance, but our schedule was such that it didn't happen.

On Monday night, as Grace and I shared supper, the serious hacking started setting in. Try as I might, I could not control it. I tried to use the inside of my sleeved elbow to smother the spread of the virus, but I shudder to think of how ineffective that was.

We climbed into bed around ten o'clock. Then things really got serious—not at all what I had hoped for. My coughing became violent. In the midst of one of those nasty coughing fits, I decided to turn over and see if I could find relief. I didn't. The opposite happened. I heard a pop, and then a sharp pain speared me in my lower left rib cage. Now I was really in trouble. I could hardly breathe, and yet the perpetual tickle raged until I gave in and coughed some more, leading to an immediate, intense, searing pain in my side.

Now in agony, I rolled out of bed to leave the room and give Grace a chance for more sleep. I spent the rest of that night pacing the floor downstairs, reclining on my La-Z-Boy, or bending over the counter and holding my side while I coughed uncontrollably.

I like to think that there is something good in everything that happens. Yes, that is probably overly optimistic, but a few days of coughing eruptions while trying to hold in the searing pain in my side has led me to do some thinking. It sobered me to realize how what happens to us has the potential to hurt us beyond the obvious. I never found out the precise cause of the pain in my side, and I was not sure which was worse, the coughing or the searing pain. All I knew is that it was not a good combination and both hurt together.

In the same way, when my actions distract me from God's love, it affects me in more ways than I can tell. And sadly, it affects others around me too.

Life is full of challenges, and there is not a "vaccine" that will protect us from all of them. But God has promised that He will never fail or abandon us (Hebrews 13:5) and that He will give us strength to face whatever comes our way (Philippians 4:13). We will not necessarily understand, and we may find God's promises hard to believe, but that doesn't change the fact that they are real and can be relied on. Life is sometimes unfair, and some people have to face more than others, but the promise is the same. So, we must carry on.

Reunion

*"Suddenly, Jesus' words flashed
through Peter's mind: 'Before the rooster
crows twice, you will deny three times that
you even know me.' And he broke down
and wept." – Mark 14:72*

The story of Peter's betrayal of Jesus prior to the crucifixion is often told. I find it very troubling to read the various biblical crucifixion accounts, as they are a reminder of the horrible price paid to ransom us, as unlovable as we are, by our Creator. I must admit I feel sorry for Peter, who wanted to go to bat for Jesus but failed. Peter seemed to be the one who was out there much more than the other disciples during the confusing events leading to Jesus' trial and conviction. In a reactionary attempt to defend Jesus from the mob, Peter even cut off the ear of a member of the posse in the Garden of Gethsemane. He would have had good reason to join the other disciples in hiding, but he put himself at further risk and followed the procession of men who were hungry for the blood of his friend, Jesus. (One of the other disciples, John, also followed Jesus into that mock court of justice, but, according to John 18:15-16, he was apparently well known by the Jewish leaders and thus not as much at risk. According to tradition, John is the only disciple who did not die a violent death.)

I can only imagine what must have been going through Peter's head. He had good reason to run for his life. In the darkness of the courtyard, in very short order, Peter denied even knowing Jesus three times. If he had been thinking clearly, he would have realized how ridiculous his denial would seem. There must have been many who would have recognized him.

I can't imagine how any of the followers of Jesus must have felt as their hopes were crushed and the reality of Jesus' prediction of His death started to settle in. I am quite sure that Jesus' further prediction of resurrection was not believed and thus His death seemed to have finality to it. It represented not only the end of Jesus' life, but also of His call to the disciples to join His kingdom of love and freedom. No wonder the remaining disciples were hiding behind a locked door, in fear for their lives (John 20:19).

When the women returned from the empty tomb to report their discovery, their story was dismissed and considered nonsense by the disciples. John 20:2-10 suggests that Peter and John were the only ones who decided to check out their story. A footrace to the tomb ensued. John won (a detail that only appears in the Gospel that he wrote!). Even though John got there first, he did not enter the tomb—until Peter, ever the brave one, arrived and entered. John's account indicates that all they saw was the folded linens in an empty tomb.

I can only imagine how much Peter wanted to see the risen Jesus. He had pledged to be with Him and had failed Him, and I am sure he wanted to apologize and seek forgiveness. But all he saw on that resurrection morning was the empty tomb. Or was it? There is a verse, hidden in another story, that reveals that Jesus must have appeared to Peter early on that day. The disciples announced to the men who had returned to Jerusalem after encountering Jesus on the road to Emmaus: "The Lord has really risen! He appeared to Peter" (Luke 24:34). I have been unable to find any other reference to the appearance of Jesus solely to Peter except for Paul's statement in 1 Corinthians 15:5: "He (the resurrected Jesus) was seen by Peter and then by the Twelve." Oh, how I would love to hear more about that reunion—maybe I will someday. I can imagine Peter falling on his knees and begging forgiveness. I can also imagine Jesus tenderly touching Peter, perhaps joining him on the ground, and explaining to him that all this had to happen to fulfill the plan of salvation. I can imagine Jesus describing how His death had provided freedom from sin, freedom from hatred, freedom from fear, and even freedom from death. Love is stronger than death, and Jesus had proved that the battle had been won.

The resurrection of Jesus is central to our faith. It must have happened. Why else would this band of followers, at first hiding out in a locked room, step out boldly to tell the Good News wherever they went? They knew that Jesus had been crucified, but they must also have seen Him risen and realized that there was little that people could now do to them. They were free from that prison that so easily confines us too.

I am not sure I understand much of that freedom. Some days I do more than other days, but the older I get, the more I am grateful for that gift. I know I am loved—always—and that is Good News!

Resurrection Sunday

"But as for me, God will redeem my life.
He will snatch me from the power
of the grave." – Psalm 49:15

When I awoke this morning, there were no robins singing to bring a smile to my face. There was no promise of sunshine for the day, as persistent dark clouds separated us from any hope of seeing blue skies anytime soon. Yet my heart was filled with joy. From somewhere deep inside me, a message came: "It is Resurrection Sunday!"

In my mind, I pictured the tomb with the stone rolled away. Light was spilling out from inside the black interior of the tomb—it could not be contained by darkness any longer. Unbelief and belief spread quickly among Jesus' bewildered followers. Questions were asked by many, but firm belief in a resurrected Jesus was hard to find.

Luke 24 reports that three days after Jesus' crucifixion, two of Jesus' followers had left Jerusalem to go to Emmaus, about a seven-mile walk. They were in deep conversation when a third party joined them and asked: "What are you discussing so intently as you walk along?"

They stopped short, "sadness written across their faces" (hardly evidence that they believed the report of a risen Jesus), and responded: "You must be the only person in Jerusalem who hasn't heard about all the things that have happened there the last few days."

"What things?" Jesus asked. I wonder if there was a bit of a smile on His face. These were likely dear friends of His who were very troubled.

They went on to describe their take on Jesus' life and their disappointment: "We had hoped he was the Messiah who had come to rescue Israel. This all happened three days ago. Then some women from our group of his followers were at his tomb early this morning, and they came back with an amazing report. They said his body was missing, and they had seen angels who told them Jesus is alive! Some of our men ran out to see, and sure enough, his body was gone, just as the women had said."

The two followers of Jesus did not say that Jesus was alive, only that his body was gone. They did not know that His risen body was now right in front of them. Once again, I wonder if a faint smile crossed Jesus' face.

Jesus began to walk them through the Scriptures as they carried on with their journey. When darkness fell, the two begged Him to stay with them for the night—an invitation which He apparently accepted. But then something dramatic happened: "As they sat down to eat, he took the bread and blessed it. Then he broke it and gave it to them. Suddenly, their eyes were opened, and they recognized him. And at that moment, he disappeared."

Suddenly the darkness of the evening no longer mattered. Within the hour, they were back on the road to Jerusalem to report to Jesus' other followers, who all said: "The Lord has really risen!"

The light was out of the tomb, never to be sealed in again. The great enemy, death, had been overcome by the resurrection, and now there was new life, just as had been promised. The Messiah had come. As Jesus had said in John 12:24: "I tell you the truth, unless a kernel of wheat is planted in the soil and dies, it remains alone. But its death will produce many new kernels—a plentiful harvest of new lives."

As I lay there in my bed on Resurrection Sunday, I thought of various family members: My grandparents—living again! Grace's Mom and Dad—alive and well! My nephew Andy—full of energy and life! Pictures of each one of them came into my mind. They were all fine. They had new life. They had been resurrected from darkness.

As I finished writing these thoughts, the sun broke through

the clouds in the east, its radiance casting long morning shadows. Like that light bursting through darkness, I recalled Jesus' words:

"Don't let your hearts be troubled" – John 14:1

"I am leaving you with a gift—peace of mind and heart.
And the peace I give is a gift the world cannot give.
So don't be troubled or afraid" – John 14:27

"I have come as light in this dark world, so that all who put their trust in me will no longer remain in the dark."
– John 12:46

Church at Home

"The Lord is my shepherd;
I have all that I need...
He guides me along right paths,
bringing honor to his name."
– Psalm 23:1, 3

"Heaven's King, who created everything,
is there something I could bring to you?"
– Noel Richards

It was Sunday morning, after two late nights in a row, and I was tempted to consider the possibility of having "church" at home this morning. We had gone for a shorter walk than usual in order to give ourselves enough time for a bowl of cereal and a cherished cup of Guatemalan coffee. While sitting at the table with Grace, I suggested that maybe we could ask God to open our hearts to His love at home this morning. He does that regularly, and perhaps this could be another one of those times. We are not as guilt-ridden about not making it to church on the weekend as we might have been in the past, but we try to attend whenever possible.

As tempting as it was to stay home this morning, that option did not seem to be the right one. I felt good about the decision and prayed that our hearts would be open that morning at church.

We joined scores of people streaming into the church at about 9:02. We are almost always at least two minutes late for any service we attend. It is likely just a bad habit or perhaps the outgrowth of a deep-seated psychological condition—but at least we know that we have lots of company. The sanctuary (an odd name if you do not feel safe in a large crowd) was festooned with flags from many nations. It was "Global Connections" weekend, celebrating the global reach of the Christian church. A couple of songs were sung, and then there was a Scripture reading in five languages. I loved that and was delighted that I could understand a lot of the Scripture read in Spanish. Maybe after all my visits to Guatemala over the years, the language is actually starting to stick.

A reading of Psalm 23 was included. A "street person," sharing the stage with the reader and contributing her interpretation of the reading out of a deep state of despair, added to the drama of that precious Psalm. Then another person came walking across the stage. Noticing the homeless person, she took off her sweater and wrapped it around the bedraggled young lady. Then she took off her shoes and placed them on the homeless person's feet. At that point, tears welled up. I wondered how many of us in the church were that aware of our privileged position and knew what to do about it.

A soloist sang a very powerful song about reaching out to others around us. It tugged at my heart, but I was saved from sliding into that place where tears come uncontrolled by a little girl sitting with her Dad. He had been a kid in our youth group when Grace and I were youth sponsors. The little girl would smile at me and then hide behind her Dad's shoulder. She was so cute, it charmed me into peace.

The worship leader led us in a song that was new to me. The words suggested that I would be willing to go anywhere to serve the King. I wondered if I could sing those words with honesty, knowing that I still hang on to so much.

By now I was well prepared for the next song. The words of the song could only be sung silently inside my soul—my physical self could not utter a word. "I bring my hands, my heart, my feet to share your love with those in need." Where had such a deep connection to these words come from? I held back the tears, but then came the line: "Use my arms to hold the lonely, let that be my song of love to you."

Tears streamed down my face. I cried out to God from a deep place of inner loneliness, that place where God meets me, and I longed for others to also feel His love. There are so many lonely people in this fallen world, stumbling along, bumping into each other, and apologizing for that connection instead of turning to embrace one another.

When I got home, I wanted to find the words to that song and record them in my journal. I tried Googling several phrases that I thought were part of the song. I had written a couple of them down after we had sung the song in church, hoping that they would be enough to help me find the complete song. But I did not have any success whatsoever.

I sat down at my computer to e-mail our worship leader and ask for his help. As I did so, I decided to put on some music and randomly chose something from the hundreds of songs on my computer. It was a Noel Richards album called *Heaven's King*.

Tears flowed down my cheeks. The first song from the album was the one that I was looking for.

"Dear Father, what did You just do?" I prayed. "Thank You for reminding me that You are with me, that You love me, and that You care for me, stumbling along on this journey."

So I had church at church and church at home today too.

A Lesson from Rhubarb

*"We can rejoice, too, when we run into problems and trials,
for we know that they help us develop endurance. And
endurance develops strength of character, and character
strengthens our confident hope of salvation. And this hope
will not lead to disappointment. For we know how dearly
God loves us, because he has given us the Holy Spirit
to fill our hearts with his love." – Romans 5:3-5*

Grace brought in a couple of stalks of fresh rhubarb this week. She had purchased a rhubarb plant for the new garden plot at our home a while back, and it had finally grown large enough to be used. The stalks were a little on the skimpy side, but nevertheless they were fresh rhubarb—a sign of spring in the Fraser Valley.

For years, we have purchased fabulous rhubarb from a neighbor to the south who has an acre or so in production. There is nothing like a good rhubarb crisp and the smell of butter, brown sugar, and oats melting together in the oven. It is best served warm with a little ice cream and a cup of serious coffee.

Rhubarb is a curious plant. It is quite hardy and faithfully delivers its bounty year after year. But is it a fruit or a vegetable? It certainly appears to be a cousin of celery, and yet I have often heard it referred to as a fruit and never as a vegetable.

After a little research, I discovered that it took a US court decision in 1946 to finally resolve the question and clarify that rhubarb should be included in the fruit category. How much sense does that make? Then I read a little more about it. I found out that even though it may not make sense, the decision did make cents for the rhubarb importers of the day. If rhubarb had been designated as a vegetable, it would have been charged higher import duties than if it were designated as a fruit. Is this really how we should make these kinds of decisions?

But I am not very interested in the politics involved. I am more interested in rhubarb as it grows in our garden, eventually finds its way into our fridge and freezer, and ultimately gets turned into some of the best-tasting desserts around. The plant grows out of a rhizome—a colony of roots similar to those that give rise to mushrooms and, interestingly, to the beautiful aspen trees of the Cariboo country. After a forest fire destroys all visible growth, aspen trees seem to be the first out of the ground, getting a head start on other tree species. Why? Because the tree is propagated by underground rhizomes that the fire does not destroy. So, here in our little garden, we have a fruit that looks like a vegetable and is also related to a tree. It is all part of the incredible order in creation.

When I was a child, I remember picking stalks of rhubarb on my grandparents' farm north of Saskatoon on the Canadian prairies. Of course, we would take a bite or two of the tart stem, but the real treat was dipping it into a bowl of sugar and enjoying the sweet and tart tastes together. I think we likely sucked off the sugar as much as anything, but we enjoyed the rhubarb as well.

From those early days, I can remember being told that the leaves were poisonous and that we should never eat them. I have lived by that rule ever since. But I still wonder about the fact that the stalk can be so good, the leaves can be poisonous, and yet they both come from the same root system. It is strange how information such as that can get stuck in my head.

God uses various ways of teaching us, and I even think He might be trying to teach me something through rhubarb. Like the stem and leaves of a rhubarb plant, joy and suffering often exist side by side in my life. It appears that I cannot live a life that is free from suffering. But, if I am willing to step back and think about it, I realize that in the midst of the suffering there is generally joy as well. And the reverse is true too. In the midst of joy, there is likely a place for suffering. They just grow together, and eradicating suffering from my life is about as likely as rhubarb producing that edible stalk without also producing the poisonous leaf.

God in the Clouds

*"Look up into the sky, and see the clouds
high above you...Do you understand how
he moves the clouds with wonderful
perfection and skill?"*
– Job 35:5; 37:16

*"And they will see the Son of Man
coming on the clouds of heaven
with power and great glory."*
– Matthew 24:30

It was a rare lazy Sunday afternoon, Mother's Day. The brunch for Grace was all cleaned up, and the kids had left after sitting outside in the glorious sunshine for a couple of hours. You could count the sunny Sundays so far this year on one hand and still have fingers left over. Grace and I hoped to go for a motorcycle ride before preparations commenced for a supper meal with my parents.

I pulled out a "zero gravity" lawn chair and parked it facing the sun. I had a BMW magazine, a book, and my journal sitting on a bench beside me. It didn't take long until Grace pulled up another "zero gravity" chair and lay down beside me. These chairs are just about perfect for sleeping anytime, let alone on a sunny Sunday afternoon.

Grace cradled a book in her arms for about two minutes, and then she was gone. I wasn't far behind her. Straggling stresses from the busyness of life seemed to keep me from falling into a deep sleep, but I certainly experienced some wonderful rest.

After a while, I opened my eyes to see a gorgeous blue sky with small white clouds drifting across it from the southeast. The sight reminded me of a time when I was a child visiting my grandparents' farm just out of Waldheim, Saskatchewan. I was lying on the grass and looking skyward with Grandpa.

"Can you see the horse, Stanny?" he asked as he pointed at an amorphous cloud.

Not wanting him to be disappointed, I said, "Yes," while trying my best to make some sense of it.

After some practice, though, I not only started to see the shapes he was seeing but could also offer up some of my own. There is training that is necessary for successful cloud watching, and training takes time. For a young fellow such as I was, lying on the grass and gazing at the sky did not always have the appeal that it would have later in life.

Today was one of those days. I could just lie there and watch the clouds lazily slip by. I remembered that it takes practice to see images in the clouds, and so I coached myself to pay attention and see what I could imagine. Grace was fast asleep, so I had the time to do whatever I wanted—watch clouds, read, or write in my journal. This afternoon, I chose cloud watching.

I guess I was out of practice, and it wasn't going all that well. Then I had an idea. I would try less to imagine an image in an actual cloud, but rather look for profiles along the periphery of a cloud outlined against the backdrop of the brilliant blue sky. The celestial wind currents would carve the edges of the clouds, and at one time I thought that I saw a pig—I thought that it was clear enough that I could draw it from memory later if I wanted to.

At some point, I decided to address God. I know that He is no more in the sky than on the earth, but it just seemed right to converse with Him a bit. I felt so much at peace, and perhaps that made this a good opportunity for a conversation focused on gratitude rather than petition. Mother's Day is a good time to offer up thanks.

A cloud approached from the south, the only one big enough to completely fill the space between the branches of the massive maples that ring our yard. When it was at center stage, something started to happen to the cloud. Some holes started forming in the cloud roughly where eyes would be. I chuckled, wondering if I would be able to imagine a face.

As it turned out, I did not have to use my imagination at all. No sooner had the dark eyes formed than the rest of the face came into absolutely clear focus.

Now, I have no idea what God looks like, but this face looked like what I would imagine Him to look like—kind of like the "pictures" of Moses that I have seen. The bottom of the cloud took on the shape of a very healthy beard. The face was incredibly clear. I looked over at Grace, wondering whether I should wake her up so she could see what was looking back at us from the sky. I think there was even a smirk on the cloudy face.

Then I remembered that I had my iPhone sitting on the bench beside me and it was equipped with a pretty good camera. I quickly slid the bar across the screen to activate the phone, located the icon for the camera application, and held it up to take a picture.

The image in the sky appeared to be camera shy. As soon as I pointed the phone in the direction of the image, it quickly started to lose its shape. I did take a picture, but only with a very good imagination could one pick out any of the facial features that had been so clear seconds earlier.

I found myself saying, "That is just like God, showing up for a bit and then disappearing." I said it almost as a joke and then cautioned myself for thinking such thoughts.

I pondered that experience for a bit. After a time, I began to think that perhaps God is not so much like clouds but like the blue sky that is always there. The clouds of life often obscure it or block it out, but life has proven that the blue is still there and will one day present itself clearly again. On this afternoon, the cloud had to reveal God to me; otherwise, I would have lost Him in the blue.

Okay, these thoughts might be a little weird and not fully formed, to say the least, but it was a very cool experience nonetheless. Maybe God was pleased to see that the book on the bench beside me was about His Son—*Jesus: A Biography from a Believer.*

Thank you, Grandpa, for teaching me how to watch the clouds.

Out of Line

"Don't copy the behavior and customs of this world,
but let God transform you into a new person
by changing the way you think.
Then you will learn to know God's will for you,
which is good and pleasing and perfect."
– Romans 12:2

It was a beautiful spring morning. I drove my familiar route to town, enjoying the kaleidoscope of color typical of spring in the Fraser Valley. In spring, there is an indescribable richness in the color of leaves as they unfold to embrace the reawakened world. Birds in song provide wonderful pleasure for us, although their motivation for singing is likely more strategic—trying to attract a mate to ensure the continuation of their species. Busy squirrels are also visible, often near where the birds nest. I suppose they, too, like eggs for breakfast. It can be a harsh world.

I slowed for a school zone, and as I rounded a corner, I noticed a group of young children. They were walking orderly in line, holding onto a rope like mountain climbers preparing for an ascent. Of course, this method is commonly used to "protect" the children by keeping them in line when it may be unsafe for them to wander freely. It probably works pretty well, or it would have been declared obsolete long ago.

This morning, though, I found myself wishing that at least one of the children would step out of line to look at a rock or a dandelion or maybe even bolt for an open field. Maybe subconsciously I felt that I was being held in some kind of prison. Perhaps it was I who was wishing for freedom and I was projecting that onto this innocent line of children.

My thoughts digressed further. I began to wonder if what we teach our children and each other is that compliance is of the greatest value in our society, of greater value even than cooperation. Compliance requires us to fall into line, based on the assumption that it would be safer for all of us if we did so. Cooperation, on the other hand, allows for differences within the context of mutual respect. Compliance would appear to be easier, but I doubt that it is a better way. What happens if we are all taught to be compliant and the "line" is not taking us to a safe place?

I was hoping that as soon as that string of children got to their destination, they would be able to run freely. I was hoping that they would be given the opportunity to exercise the healthy curiosity of their young minds.

I would love to have watched those children longer and perhaps whispered into some of those little ears, "Just step out of line a bit." But if I were the teacher responsible for that group, I would likely have disciplined anyone who suggested such a thing. The irony is that I think many people would feel the same way I did. Why is it that at Christmas programs we all seem to cheer for the wee one who steps out of line? It must give us hope or something—and yet what we wish for children we seem to be afraid to claim for ourselves.

I wondered if I, too, depend on being in line to secure my own ease in life. Am I afraid for some reason to explore options, perhaps even lazy, as staying in line certainly requires less work? How much of the mystery and beauty of life do I miss out on because I am "on assignment," compliant, committed to staying in line?

I think that we would be much healthier as a society if we could learn that cooperation, leaving room for each other, is likely better in the long haul than compliance. Both are important, of course, but maybe stepping out of line a little more often might provide a better world for us all.

A Hummingbird and
a Glass Wall

"But Jesus spoke to them at once.
'Don't be afraid,' he said.
'Take courage. I am here!'"
– Matthew 14:27

It was the long weekend in May—our first time up at Forest Dreams, our cabin in British Columbia's Cariboo country, since the depths of winter. Spring was lurking in the woods in the Cariboo, but it was far behind what was happening in the more temperate Fraser Valley. Even there, spring had arrived a month late this year, after a long winter. It was one of at least three long winters in a row, which may perhaps confound the "wise" among us, who are bent on seeing evidence of global warming everywhere. My thoughts turned to 1 Corinthians 1:27-29: "God chose things the world considers foolish to shame those who think they are wise. And he chose things that are powerless to shame those who are powerful. God chose things despised by the world, things counted as nothing at all, and used them to bring to nothing what the world considers important. As a result, no one can ever boast in the presence of God."

We left Abbotsford in the afternoon, giving us enough time to pick up a take-out Chinese food supper from TJ's in the small community of 100 Mile House. This has become a family tradition, which we share with our son Ryan, daughter-in-law Nathania, and their children Asia, Ethan, and Myra. After supper and a short stay at Ryan and Nathania's place, we arrived at Forest Dreams around 9:00 p.m. It felt good to get out of the truck and breathe in the wonderful fresh air. The stars were already starting to pierce the night sky. We had seen pussy willows along Madden Road just before our gate. As soon as the truck stopped, our dog Coco stood up on the back seat, stretched, sniffed the air, and clambered out of the truck, her tail wagging. She, too, loves to be here.

It didn't take us long to get unpacked and climb into bed. We were very tired from the busyness of life in the Fraser Valley. We slept well and woke to a gorgeous Cariboo morning. I smiled as I looked out the window and saw the barren trees sprouting brave little buds—a promise that things would change very soon.

As is now customary, I took the dog for a short walk down our driveway. When we returned, Grace was ready to go for a longer walk in the woods. It felt good to be embraced by God's love—He seems very close to us in this place in the Cariboo.

By the time we got back, the cabin was toasty warm from the morning sun radiating through the multitude of windows. The pot for porridge was put on the stove, and the Starbuck's espresso machine was turned on—breakfast would be ready in minutes.

We sat on the Adirondack chairs just outside the kitchen, facing the morning sun. Our coffee cups were steaming on the chair arms, and each of us was cradling a warm bowl of oatmeal, with a little maple syrup on top. The dog was filled with delight as she sniffed the air for any hint of animal life to chase back into the woods. Such moments cannot be described in words—they can at best be felt. If you have felt a similar moment, then there may be a chance that my words can awaken that memory.

After breakfast, I went into the workshop adjacent to our cabin. It, too, has many windows facing south, allowing the morning sun to warm up the air inside. I was working at something on the workbench while Grace was outside strategizing on where to start with the yard work. In the background, I could hear a fluttering sound up against the south-facing window. I assumed it was a moth or early spring wasp that had mistakenly followed me into the workshop. I would take care of that in a moment, but for now I was content to be doing what I was doing.

Grace's excited words brought my head up: "A hummingbird!"

There was still a pile of snow along our driveway. What was a hummingbird doing here this early in spring?

"Where?" I asked.

"In the shop, up against the window!"

Sure enough, three feet from me, a hummingbird was trying desperately to escape through the glass window to find freedom on the other side. He was trapped. If we had not been present, he would likely have killed himself trying to get out. The only hope that hummingbird had was to accept help from us. I was already concerned that perhaps he had hurt himself as he had flown up and down the glass pane with a recklessness born of panic.

I was not sure what to do. For a moment, I wished that Ryan was there, as he had caught a hummingbird in a similar situation when he was a young boy. I pulled the stuff away from the window sill that was sheltering the bird from my grasping hands. I fully expected that this would cause even greater panic, but the opposite happened. The hummingbird was sitting motionless, wings spread out against the glass.

I decided that I was going to try to catch the bird with my bare hand. That is what Ryan had done. I looked at the long, spear-like beak and for a moment imagined that the hummingbird could do some damage with that if he chose to. I also realized that if I panicked, I could easily do the bird harm.

I put all other considerations aside, as I knew that they would interfere with my main purpose—to help the hummingbird find his freedom. With deliberateness and resolve, I eased my hand up to the bird. To my shock, he stayed stationary, allowing me to close my bare hand gently around his frail body. He didn't even fight back.

I held that hummingbird with great care and tenderness, aware that I was holding one of God's magnificent creations in all its frailty and beauty. I brought the hummingbird outside—there was still not one bit of struggle from him—and showed him to Grace. Feeling no struggle, I wondered if he was injured.

It was time to find out. I opened my hand to lift the hummingbird up to a branch of a pine tree. To our surprise, he took off, flying away after circling back once to say good-bye.

We were very pleased to see the hummingbird flying as he was created to do—a marvelous creature, to say the least. We were thankful and amazed that he had trusted us. Even though he had had to be confined in the palm of my hand for a few minutes, somehow he seemed to know that we wanted freedom for him as much as he wanted it for himself. He had beaten himself up against that glass window for long enough, and perhaps that had caused him to trust me. Who knows? What I am quite certain of is that he would have died trying to get to freedom on his own. He needed intervention, and he had had to trust that that intervention would get him where he wanted to go. For a few moments, that intervention appeared to have taken away all of his freedom—only his head had not been in the grip of my hand. If he fought my hold on him, he would have done himself more harm. He had to completely let go, trusting me absolutely.

The application to my life is so clear in this story. In fact, it represents the story of humanity. We know that there is more to life beyond where we are. At times, we can see it, sense it, and yet we cannot seem to get there. Try as we may, we fail, until finally we are either too injured or too exhausted and we lose sight of the possibility of that place of freedom existing. It is only at that time—when we feel so alone, so tired, so hopeless—that we will let God close His hand around us and trust that He will not harm us. I am sure that the hummingbird had never had this happen to him before, and I can only imagine how frightened he was. Can the same be true of us with God? The confinement scares us, and we desperately want to get out of His hand and back to the world that we know—the world of illusion where we believe that we are the masters of our own destiny. We are not mistaken about the existence of a place where we will be what we were meant to be, a place of freedom and joy, but the glass wall that separates us from it does not appear to have any openings that would allow us to get there. Try as we may, we cannot get through on our own.

Can I be still and let God close His hand around me, trusting that He will deliver me to that place that I know exists? And is it possible that that place actually exists even here, where I live, in this life on earth, and that I can be transported periodically to it from time to time? Yes, I may have to leave my physical body behind, but can my soul be carried to that place and finally find the freedom that God wants for us all? Love wants to set us free, as we were created to be.

There is so much in the stories unfolding around us. I love how God teaches me, using so many different methods. I love that His created order and beauty seem to be my classroom at this stage of my life.

The next day, a hummingbird came to the same spot by the workshop and buzzed around us for a bit before disappearing into the forest again.

Because He Bends Down to Listen

*"I am praying to you because I know you will answer, O God.
Bend down and listen as I pray." – Psalm 17:6*

Children can draw out the best—and sometimes the worst—in us. Being near to them can release an innocence and profound sense of love—when we have time to be embraced by the moment. But that is not always the case. There are plenty of challenges that arise as well when children learn to assert themselves. Learning often happens by us "bouncing off" each other, and that can hurt too.

There are times when we encounter a child—or an elderly person driven closer to the ground by age—when we literally have to "bend down" to hear that person speak. It can be a very endearing moment for both parties. The "lesser" can feel incredibly valued as the other bends down and love connects two hearts.

I have often wondered about the God of great love who also is the one to be "feared." How does that fit together? I cannot answer that very well, but recently Grace and I have been reading a study on Job, and I think that there may be some answers there. It struck us that, although Job seemed to recognize God as judge, he also believed that that same judge would be his redeemer:

> *But as for me, I know that my Redeemer lives,*
> *and he will stand upon the earth at last.*
> *And after my body has decayed,*
> *yet in my body I will see God!*

I will see him for myself.
Yes, I will see him with my own eyes.
I am overwhelmed at the thought!
– Job 19:25-27

God as redeemer, the one who will recover possession and ownership of us, His children—that is an incredible thought!

The other day, I found a couple of related verses in Psalm 116:1-2:

I love the Lord because he hears my voice
and my prayer for mercy.
Because he bends down to listen,
I will pray as long as I have breath!

Notice the start of verse 2: "He bends down to listen." What an incredible image! God bends down to listen to us. He loves us, bending down to hear us and cherish us. As His children, can we look up at Him with great joy and trust, knowing that He can be our redeemer? There is so much chaos and confusion in life, but one fact remains—we are loved!

Doctor Francisco and his daughter Jazmin in Guatemala

A Flashlight

*"What is the price of two sparrows—one copper coin? But
not a single sparrow can fall to the ground without your
Father knowing it. And the very hairs on your head are all
numbered. So don't be afraid; you are more valuable to God
than a whole flock of sparrows." – Matthew 10:29-31*

It was a gorgeous Friday evening. We had arrived at our North
Vancouver condo in the late afternoon. This would give Grace
enough time to get her hair cut and give us a chance to get our
cruiser pedal bikes out of the storage locker. We wanted to clean
the bikes and get them ready for our son Jared. On Sunday, he
was planning on surprising his girlfriend Sonja with a visit to
Vancouver and a ride around the spectacular Stanley Park seawall
in celebration of her birthday.

The locker was a bit crowded, so we pulled some old chairs
out to take to the Salvation Army thrift store down the alley.
After shifting a few more items, we got to our two bikes, locked
together with a cable and a combination lock. The fluorescent
tube above our locker was almost burned out and was flickering
frustratingly, but it was all the light we had. I suggested to Grace
that perhaps I should take a look up in our suite to see if we had a
flashlight. We did manage to drag the bikes out of the locker into
the corridor, to take advantage of light down the aisle. Fortunately,
we remembered the combination number—it helps to program in
a phone number—and pulled the cable off. We still had to clean
the bikes and pump up the tires, but that could be done tomorrow.
Tonight we wanted to go out for supper to celebrate my birthday
from earlier in the week.

Grace left the storage locker to go across the street to have her hair done, and I returned to our suite to look for a flashlight. No luck. Oh well, I thought. We could pick one up at Walmart on the way back from supper.

We were very tired from a busy week, but both of us were looking forward to supper out on such a wonderful evening. There are lots of restaurants that offer outside dining. We chose Milestones in the newer section of the Park Royal shopping center, not far from our condo. This particular section of the mall fronted on an internal street with benches and water features.

Parking can be a challenge, especially on a Friday night, so we elected to park in a back parking lot and walk to the restaurant. The walk would also do us good.

After a great supper (red curry with chicken for both of us), we wandered around, poking our heads in and out of various businesses and enjoying the time together. Finally, we headed towards our parked car to go home. It was almost 9:00, and both of us were getting tired.

I started the vehicle, put it in reverse, and began to back out of the parking spot. I could not believe my eyes.

"Grace, is that a flashlight?" I was looking at a blue cylinder lying under where our car had been parked.

"I think so," Grace said as she got out to take a look.

She came back with a flashlight in her hand. I think both of us were very surprised when she pressed the button and the light came on. We now had the flashlight that we needed.

We laughed as we drove back to the condo, thanking God for this comical and yet beautiful event. What were the chances of us finding a flashlight under our car? It had not been there when we had pulled into the parking spot.

We now have it sitting in the locker at our condo, a very special flashlight.

I guess if God knows the number of hairs on our heads—which is becoming easier and easier in my case with each passing year—and sees the sparrow fall, He can also make a flashlight show up under our car.

It was a birthday to remember in many ways.

Weeds, Wheat, and the Dandelion

"The miracles of nature do not seem miracles because they are so common. If no one had ever seen a flower, even a dandelion would be the most startling event in the world." – Anonymous

For about two weeks in early spring every year, our field is alive with the golden color of dandelions. We are often in Guatemala when they are in their glory. When we return home, we start the battle to rid the lawn of them, using chemical sprays and digging them out by the roots. Of course, we have made little progress, as the field produces millions of seeds ready to invade our lawn whenever a wind provides an opening.

This spring was different. We arrived back from Guatemala a little earlier than usual, which gave us an opportunity to see the peak of the dandelion bloom. It was breathtaking. I took several pictures, wondering if some day people might be willing to travel great distances to see this phenomenon. I realize that would only happen if the dandelion's designation as a stubborn weed was changed to that of a flower.

One can find plenty of stories on the Internet suggesting that the dandelion has been completely misunderstood. It is a plant rich in all kinds of nutrients and is totally nonpoisonous. Its leaves can be used for food, its flowers for wine, and its roots for medicine. My grandfather would probably roll over in his grave if he knew I was offering even a little support for the dandelion, seeing beauty in the existence of the tenacious Taraxacum, as it is officially named. Or maybe not. An online poll saw only thirteen percent of respondents classifying the dandelion as a pesky weed—the others saw it as beneficial. A farmer might suggest that it is obvious a majority of those responding to the poll have never had to duke it out with dandelions in their fields every spring.

I am still not sure that I won't continue my battle with the dandelions in my yard, but perhaps with a bit more hesitation. Perhaps there is room for them to grow alongside what we consider to be more worthy plants—not that we have any say in the matter anyway.

My thoughts turned to a parable that Jesus taught to a crowd of people in Matthew 13:24-29. It appears that the crowd had gathered not far from Jesus' home in Capernaum along the shores of the Sea of Galilee. A lot of people in the area were employed in farming, and Jesus, typically, used the language of the people to tell a story. I assume that many grain farmers were in the audience that day.

Jesus started His parable this way: "The Kingdom of Heaven is like a farmer who planted good seed in his field." If I were a farmer, I would have been paying close attention, wondering where He was going to go with this story. After all, Jesus had just told the story of the reckless farmer who cast his seed all over the place, and the farmers in the crowd were probably still thinking about the meaning of that one. This time, while the workers were asleep, the farmer's enemy planted weeds among the wheat and slipped away. As a farmer listening to this story, I would likely have seen this as very troubling and would have been thinking that the farmer should get his workers to pull those weeds out as quickly as possible.

But that is not how Jesus' story went. When the crew asked  the farmer if they should pull the weeds out, the farmer responded: "No, you'll uproot the wheat if you do. Let both grow together until the harvest. Then I will tell the harvesters to sort out the weeds, tie them into bundles, and burn them, and to put the wheat in the barn."

When we were kids, my siblings and I had to weed our family garden. Mom never gave us the option of leaving the weeds to grow alongside the veggies until they matured. We had to pull the weeds to save the harvest.

I have thought a lot about that parable. Later in the chapter, when the crowds were "outside," the disciples privately asked Jesus to explain this parable (Matthew 13:36-43). Jesus responded by first identifying the farmer as the Son of Man, a title that He used to refer to Himself. The field is the world, the good seed represents the people of the Kingdom of Heaven, and the weeds are the people of the evil one. The enemy who planted the weeds is the devil, the harvest is the end of the world, and the harvesters are the angels.

It appears that the weeds will always exist alongside the wheat in our life here on earth. It also appears that God will allow the weeds and the wheat to grow together—at least until it is time for the harvest. While they are still on earth, the people of the Kingdom of Heaven will always exist and grow in the presence of the weeds of the evil one. We will compete for the same limited resources of water, sunshine, and nutrients. And, surprisingly, our job is not to pull out what we think are the weeds, but rather to leave that to the farmer.

Can we read into this parable that we have to be willing to live alongside people of all kinds, of all faiths, of every orientation, sharing the same field—and to allow God to reap the harvest when the time comes?

It may be possible that, as a tiny stalk of wheat, I cannot necessarily determine the identity of the plant growing beside me. I may look for differences rather than similarities and conclude prematurely that that neighboring plant is an enemy. Perhaps what I decide is a weed may actually turn into wheat of another variety if given time to grow.

I know that there is plenty of teaching in the Scripture about the church keeping itself pure, but does this parable also apply? I guess that I need to trust the farmer more than my own judgment.

And I have learned to respect the dandelions growing in my field as well. Since arriving back from Guatemala, I have harvested dandelion leaves to make tea (it did not taste too bad). And Grace has harvested a healthy collection of stinging nettle leaves to be used for a variety of purposes. I suppose I should be grateful that we do not live in a weed-free environment. Who knows? It might not be long before I would miss my fields of gold in the spring. If I don't have to launch an all-out war against the dandelions every spring—one that I cannot win anyway—perhaps I can live a gentler existence in this field we call life. Perhaps I can learn to see beauty where once I saw weeds and work.

We Are in This Together

"No man is an island, entire of itself...any man's death diminishes me, because I am involved in mankind." – John Donne

"I am a part of all that I have met."
– Alfred, Lord Tennyson

We arrived at church about thirty seconds before the service started. I had already complained to Grace on the drive in that we were going to get to church early. She answered: "Are we there yet?" We weren't, so she had a good point. But I reminded her when we got there that I had been right. She might argue that we were less than thirty seconds early, but the important point is that we were early. I have no idea why that is an important point.

We managed to find seats in the back row, in a section that was not roped off for latecomers—which is the section we have usually sat in for most of our twenty plus years of attending this church. I guess when you settle into a section, that is where you sit—and you expect others to do the same. I have often looked over the various sections and taken note of those who were there, in the same places, week in and week out. For whatever reason, the church leaders chose "our" section, the section where we have sat for decades, as the latecomer section, not open to the public until after the start of the service. Of course, that is only of concern on those days when we arrive "early," which was the case this day.

Once we had settled into our seats, we became very aware of three people sitting directly in front of us. There was an elderly lady—I guess in her eighties—sitting beside a very tough-looking young guy in his twenties. Beside him was a very pretty young woman with long blonde hair, likely in her twenties as well. She appeared very burdened. The guy had a ball cap on backwards and pulled to the side—the "gangster" or "bad boy" look. We noticed that his physical presence supported that image when he stood up for the singing portion of the service. Tattoos ran up and down his obviously well-developed arms.

As the service progressed, the young woman purposefully looked over at him, apparently hoping that he would return the glance. No way! He stood with his arms crossed and pulled into his chest. You could feel her pleading with her eyes, but to no avail. The hurt in her eyes was unmistakable.

During the time of greeting one another, since we were in the back row, we had no others to shake hands with and greet but them—which was fine with us. We said hello and got their first names, and then the service resumed.

At one point during the singing, the young woman got up enough courage to position herself beside the guy and actually attempt to hold his hand. There was no giving in on his part. She ended up more or less holding his elbow. It was very painful to watch. As tears started welling up in my eyes, I noticed Grace going for her purse to get a kleenex. She, too, was very saddened by the "story" we were observing. I prayed that somehow God would enter this place, enter their lives, and touch them with His love. I felt that the young man's crossed arms were meant to keep all love out, but I prayed that God would find a way in.

Grace and I talked later of how profoundly we were both impacted by what we had seen and how it had burdened us to the point of tears. Our son Jared and his wife Sonja were sitting beside us, and Sonja commented that she had been motivated to pray for the young couple as well. We may never see them again, but the pain we felt was very real and very deep. When a human suffers, others do as well—and not just those who know the sufferer. As Paul said in Philippians 1:30, "We are in this struggle together."

I am unlikely to ever see these two young adults again, but I will continue to pray for them. I believe that one of the reasons—perhaps the best one—for getting to church early that day was to sit behind them.

The Crow Strategy
and a Warning

"Be still in the presence of the Lord,
and wait patiently for him to act."
– Psalm 37:7

The Dawn Chorus—I had never heard that term until recently. But I have been a fan of the reality for years, even though I didn't know what it was called. About half an hour before sunrise, there is often an incredibly intense bird choir, with each bird seemingly trying to outdo the others with its singing. The sound typically quiets before actual sunrise. On warm nights, we sleep with the outside door of our bedroom open. It is a great idea for allowing the cool evening breeze to flow in, but not such a good idea if one wants to sleep soundly until sunrise!

On our return home from one of our morning walks, we passed a huge maple tree, where a bird cacophony caught our attention. The noise seemed even more intense than a typical dawn chorus, and it was about three hours later than usual. What we saw was quite disturbing.

A crow, out looking for breakfast, had decided to steal a fledgling bird from its nest. The birds in the vicinity would not allow such an invasion without protest, and we were surprised at the platoon of birds that began chasing that crow through the tangle of branches. A mourning dove even joined the much smaller robins, sparrows, and swallows in pursuit of the crow. They were all intent on protecting the vulnerable hatchling as if it was their own. The crow finally escaped the tree and fled—but only for a moment. He circled around, still being pursued, and headed straight back to the tree. His first, scouting trip had revealed the location of the nest. This time, he grabbed a little bird on the fly and sped off, the little one hanging helplessly from his beak. It upset us quite a bit as we watched the futile pursuit by the army of birds, all much smaller than the crow. I wished I had my pellet gun with me, so I could put an end to this. But the crow has to eat too.

As the crow flew off, still pursued by the mixed flock, we were further dismayed to see another crow perched strategically nearby. He quickly swooped in and helped himself to another baby bird, encountering very little resistance since the masses were gone, caught up in their futile chase of the first crow.

Nature can be very harsh, but on this morning it also showed that differences matter little in the presence of a common enemy. The other birds had united, seeing that the crow was a threat to them all. It was also sobering to realize that their united action had left the vulnerable more exposed to further threats.

So, in life, how do we know when it is useful to band together for the common good in the face of a threat? How do we know when it is wise to abandon the immediate threat and look at the big picture in order to prevent even more destruction? There are plenty of needs among us, calling us to pursue them, but is there also a danger of jumping onto a bandwagon and leaving the ones we are trying to protect even more vulnerable? Our intentions may be good, but sometimes the result may be the opposite of what we intended.

Psalm 37:7 advises us, "Be still in the presence of the Lord, and wait patiently for him to act." But that is hard to do sometimes!

Finding My Way Home

"Men go abroad to wonder at the heights of mountains, at the huge waves of the sea, at the long courses of the rivers, at the vast compass of the ocean, at the circular motions of the stars, and they pass by themselves without wondering." – St. Augustine

On a recent walk in North Vancouver, Grace and I came across a civic exhibit promoting an active lifestyle. Several colorful booths were set up in front of the city hall with very healthy people gathered around them. Some were wearing badges and handing out information on various trails in the area.

We struck up a conversation with a director of recreation from West Vancouver, and she said something that has stuck with me. We were talking about the new Green Necklace urban greenway under development in the Central Lonsdale area of North Vancouver, and she invited us to join a walk scheduled for that location later in the day. She was hoping to inspire quite a number of people to join the walk, which would give the trail some exposure to the public. The walk was to be about two kilometers in length.

I think I said something about a walk like that likely being quite acceptable to many.

Her answer surprised me. She said that it is difficult to get people to go on walks in general.

I asked what she saw as the greatest barrier to people joining a walk.

Her answer: "Many people are afraid that they will not make it back home."

I found that hard to believe at first, but the more we talked

about it, the more I believed that she was correct. If one has not walked—and by that I mean walked at places other than a shopping mall for any distance at all—the idea of walking two kilometers could be unnerving. It is not because the distance is that great, as I am sure many people walk at least that much on any given day. But, for people who have not done it and are not familiar with what it means, the idea alone could conjure up a mental picture of possible defeat. I would think that, for most people, a single experience of going on a two-kilometer walk would be all that it would take to put their minds at ease. It might even prove to them that a walk can be enjoyable.

As I have spent time thinking that through, I have become aware that I have had similar fears in my own life. There have been times in my life when I have been hesitant to leave the given and the known. I have been reluctant to take risks, whether it be in a recreational pursuit, a social gathering, or some other generally harmless experience.

But I also reached the conclusion that I have become quite at peace—something not always the case in my life—and I am delighted to be in this stage of life. I wonder if perhaps I am finding "home" inside me and I am able to take that home wherever I go. Now, I am not perfectly consistent with this, but I seem to be more and more comfortable wherever I may find myself. Of course, this does not cause me to climb ridiculous mountains—or even hills— but it allows me to take other risks and not feel as fearful.

For many years, our family has enjoyed numerous camping experiences. We had a little trailer, then a tent trailer, and then, of course, a Volkswagen van—all of this was when we were attending university and were as poor as church mice. None of these had any great value—I think we paid $800 for the trailer and around $1500 for the van—but they allowed us to explore the great outdoors while dragging our physical home with us. Not many years of our life have passed without us having a portable home of some sort. Oddly enough, in the last few years, we have added real, permanent homes in places that we love to be.

I think I still have a lot of work to do to feel confident that my home is in me. Maybe I just get glimpses of the possibility every now and then. I don't think it is me anyway. Rather, I think that feeling of home is the place where God dwells within me and waits for me to arrive. It is the place where I really do feel at peace and completely loved.

This reminds me of the story of Jesus' transfiguration in Matthew 17:1-15. Jesus chose three of His disciples to climb up a high mountain to be alone with Him—Peter, James, and John. I guess at least they had a healer with them if they went into cardiac arrest. When they arrived on the mountain, Jesus' physical appearance shocked them because He shone like the sun. The next minute, two more men showed up—Elijah and Moses. I have no idea how they were identified, as none of the disciples had ever seen them before. Jesus seemed to be in conversation with them in His brilliant state, talking about His death and exit from this world. It was a topic that the disciples did not welcome. Peter's efforts to confront Jesus about this earlier had not gone well, as Jesus had seemed to call him "Satan." (That story is in Matthew 16.) Then, to top off the experience, a bright cloud appeared overhead, and a voice rattled their already frightened spirits: "This is my dearly loved Son, who brings me great joy. Listen to him."

This was too much for the disciples, who fell facedown to the ground. Who knows what they thought would happen? Maybe they thought they were all about to be struck dead.

Then comes verse 7, the verse I love: "Jesus came over and touched them. 'Get up,' he said. 'Don't be afraid.' And when they looked, Moses and Elijah were gone, and they saw only Jesus."

As I live my life, beset with so much uncertainty and selfishness, two of the many things that lead to fear, I hope that I will find myself at home more and more, that I will find myself more often in that place of love and communion. I hope, when I am bent over in fear, that I will know the touch of Jesus and look up to see only Him. That indeed will feel like home. I hope that I will learn to spend more and more time with myself, accepting the beauty of God's creation in me. That statement seems as ridiculous to write as it does to believe.

I doubt if I will ever live my life feeling completely at home. Perhaps I may always wonder, too, whether I will find my way to my final home. But, at the end of the day, that decision has already been made. As a child of God, loved by God, I can be confident that I will find my way home. Maybe more correctly, I can be confident that I will be carried home.

Roundabouts and God

*"So God led them in a roundabout way through
the wilderness." – Exodus 13:18*

A few months ago, I drove the new, highly publicized McCallum
Road roundabout, which "controls" a major intersection in
our community of Abbotsford. This marvel of modern traffic
studies and engineering—imported from England and France,
the latter boasting more than half of the world's roundabouts—
has been introduced to our society over the last decade or so.
Roundabouts existed in our area before, but traditionally in quiet
neighborhoods, where traffic generally meandered along anyway.
Now they are sprouting up as safer, "traffic calming" alternatives
at busy intersections.

Roundabouts call for a major change in the way we drive. They
require a much different approach than the old intersections we
have become accustomed to since we were kids. The uncontrolled
intersection, initially governed by courtesy, worked for years.
Then we became more enlightened and developed the controlled
intersection, where stop signs and eventually traffic lights took the
place of courtesy. This was really the only reasonable alternative
as the volumes of traffic skyrocketed and road rage became more
common. I can well remember trips to church on Sunday morning;
sanctification apparently didn't include the time spent piloting
a high-speed automobile to make sure that we got to church on
time. But that is another story.

Back to the issue of roundabouts. I had cut my roundabout-
driving teeth on the Mt. Lehman roundabout that had already been
in operation for a couple of years. It is in a high traffic area that I

frequent. But that little Mt. Lehman traffic calming device is about to get a major test in a few months, as one of the largest malls in the province of British Columbia opens alongside it. Next Christmas, I think I will sit there with a camera and record some YouTube videos. 'Tis the season to be jolly, and I am sure what I record will provide a lot of laughs at others' expense. I know that is not what was intended by the well-meaning engineers who designed the roundabout, but I have confidence in the predictability of human behavior.

Regarding the McCallum Road roundabout, I am not sure what caused me to even consider attempting this route. I think it was like the call of the sirens—I was helpless to resist. I entered from the east and was immediately shocked by a sign that looked like a massive starburst, each ray of the star labeled with the name of a road. I slammed on the brakes to try to read a couple of the directions. I had not even seen the sign until I was almost there, making me wonder what it would be like on a dark and stormy night—we get plenty of those here in British Columbia. I managed to read one or two directions and then looked in my mirror. Oh, no! A seasoned driver was right behind me, and the look on his face was not good. I let go of the brake, and in a second I was under the sign with little idea of where I was going to go.

No sooner had I chosen an exit—after looking over my shoulder on my right, then looking over my shoulder on my left and checking all my mirrors and everywhere else I could think of—than I was dumped into another roundabout! I managed to find an escape route and finally caught my breath. What had just happened?

I got up enough courage to try again at a later date, and fortunately this time there was less traffic. I had more time and was prepared for the starburst sign. That sign indicated at least five choices in the little roundabout—you take the wrong one and you end up on your way to Hope far to the east or, worse, in a parking lot for our local new entertainment and sports center. It is about a kilometer away, and, on foot, you will be lucky to arrive at the center alive on a dark and stormy night after parking your car. But, since there is only parking for 300 cars on site for the 8,000 seats, you have to take what you can get. Likely the parking plan was devised by the same engineers who worked on the traffic patterns for the area.

I guess the good thing about the center island in the roundabout is that it has a sculpture of sorts, with metal replicas of salmon hanging off it. It is a welcome diversion for those who are trapped in the inner lane, not knowing that they have the right of way to do anything they want. They can occupy the time they spend stalled indecisively in the roundabout by absorbing the beauty of the sculpture and wondering what salmon have to do with McCallum Road.

I still use that roundabout once in a while. Before entering, I prepare myself to look for the humor in the venture. You can see some panicky drivers entering the circle, hunched over the wheel of their vehicles, as they timidly slip into the vortex. Others put on the intimidating ugly face that tells everyone to get out of their way or else. I know an elderly man who entered a roundabout and exited going back in the direction he had come from without even knowing it. He thought he had followed straight through. It took a lot to convince him otherwise before he was willing to head into it and try again.

This morning, I was reading in Exodus 13 about the Israelites fleeing Egypt. Verse 18 says, "God led them in a roundabout way..." God used the roundabout approach to lead His people to freedom. Now if we could just have a cloud by day and fire by night to lead us, perhaps we could learn to follow the roundabout too.

There is a story in there too. I am sure many of us live our lives in a roundabout way. Perhaps that is because God loves us and, as He did with the Israelites, He uses the roundabouts to protect us. If the Israelites had taken the most direct route, they would have gone through Philistia, which was very unfriendly territory. The roundabout way just might have protected them from hardships and sufferings beyond those that they did experience.

Don't get me wrong. I am not yet convinced that the modern-day roundabout is a keeper. Like many things, it has been forced upon us, and we will adapt. But my generation will likely have to pass away before it becomes a "traffic calming" device. Maybe that is why the Israelites had to wander around for forty years—to get rid of the old generation.

Just the Right Nut

"Whatever is good and perfect is a gift coming down to us from God our Father, who created all the lights in the heavens." – James 1:17

It was a wet Saturday morning at the condo in North Vancouver. Across Burrard Inlet, downtown Vancouver was more or less hidden behind a curtain of fog. It was not cold this morning, but I was wishing for a little more sunshine.

It was time to walk the dog. She always seems oblivious to the weather—unless it is the middle of a rare heat wave. We put on our well-used rain gear. A ball cap keeps the rain from dripping off the hoods of our jackets and onto our faces.

We chose to exit at the back of the building, emerging onto a paved lane. The dog was pulling on her leash by now, a bit anxious to get to that patch of grass that she and many other dogs have used many times.

The rain caused us to look downward. There is generally not much to see on the ground in a paved alley in the city. But this time I noticed a hex nut lying by a little puddle. I smiled and felt that it was a gift for us this morning. Could a hex nut lying in an alley in the rain be considered a gift? In this case, yes, it could.

The day before, we had had to move a marble slab table off our deck and into our suite. There had been concerns about moisture leakage in our condo building, and the decks needed to be checked out. The ceramic tile would have to be removed from the decks and remedial work done as necessary. Our table would be used as a workbench by the construction workers, and we had decided it would be best to move it inside in preparation for the work to be done.

It is a fairly heavy table, and Grace agreed to help me bring it into the suite. When we tried to lift it by the top, one side of the table came off the heavy base. I looked underneath and discovered that one of the inset bolts was missing a nut and thus the tabletop was unattached at that point. I made a note to remove one of the sister hex nuts and take it to the hardware store to find a replacement, knowing that threads can be different from one hex nut to another. With a little extra care, we moved the table inside.

Back to the following day, Saturday, and our walk in the alley. I bent over, picked up the hex nut, and said to Grace, "A gift for this morning." She knew right away what I was hoping. It was highly unlikely because our suite is four floors above the alley and there is lots of traffic in the lane as well. But it sure looked like it might be the one.

Upon our return to our suite, I lay on the floor under the table, now in our living room, and attempted to put the nut on the bolt. It was a perfect fit, identical to the other ones still present! I am not sure if it was the exact one—that would have been amazing because it would have had to have been out in that lane for a few weeks—but it fit perfectly.

I was amazed that I had found just the right nut. I will accept it as a playful gift from our heavenly Father on a wet Saturday morning. Something like that makes the simple seem so spiritual. That suits me just fine.

Of Shipping Containers, Caves, and Light

"Put your trust in the light while there is still time; then you will become children of the light." – John 12:36

Everywhere there were hills over 6,000 feet above sea level. The area reminded us of our trips to Guatemala, but we were actually in the Sierra Nevadas in central California. We were here because this was the location of Hume Lake Camp, a Christian facility providing adventure to over 2,000 kids a week during the summer. There seemed to be the potential for injury literally around every corner, and we wondered how risk management was handled in an environment like this.

We were being given a tour by Fletcher and Alli Klassen, who had been part of the program and worked here for years. They had invited us to spend three nights with them at the camp after we had joined family and friends for a reception in celebration of their marriage, which had occurred around Christmas time of the previous year.

Fletch said there was a cave that he wanted to show us. He took us out to the camping area dedicated to the grade four to six kids, pointed to a dome, and said, "This is it." A shipping container had been buried under the dome of piled earth, creating a manmade cave. The first entrance we saw was a culvert piercing the side of the hill maybe thirty inches in diameter. We knelt down to peer into the darkness and decided that there was no way we were crawling into that orifice. It was pitch black inside. Who knows what we might meet there?

Fletch ran up the rest of the hill and disappeared. We followed him and found an entrance into what appeared to be an old mine shaft. It was about four-and-a-half feet in height—perfect for kids, but not so much for me. Grace could quite easily hunch over and progress down the shaft, using her cell phone for light. I tried to activate mine, but for some reason the flashlight would not work. I punched at my phone, as if to blame it for the lack of light, but it still wouldn't turn on. I followed the limited light ahead, at one point banging my head on a beam, all the while fighting a pressing desire to turn back.

The shaft emptied into the shipping container, where Fletch was calmly perched on a ledge. It was really quite amazing. I finally got my phone flashlight to work and scanned the cave. There were bookshelves along one of the walls. I wondered how many animals had considered using this prefab home for themselves— and whether any of them could still be hiding in the dark corners. Rattlesnakes are not uncommon around the camp.

It was time to leave. Fletch scurried out the culvert exit, with Grace following right behind. Now it was my choice. I could go back the way I had entered, or I could get down on my hands and knees and exit behind Grace, who was already out of sight. I think the distance to travel was less than thirty feet, but the daylight at the end of the culvert seemed distant. Generally, culverts don't get narrower, so, in spite of the way it looked, off I went, scrambling on my hands and knees. I realized that, if for some reason I changed my mind in the middle of the culvert, I could not back up. The only way out was to keep going toward the light.

It only took a few seconds before I was able to crawl out onto the ground and rise to my feet, but it had seemed like much longer.

Then a thought came. Life is full of challenges, darkness, and uncertainty. The only way out is to continue to keep our eyes fixed on the light. Our journey will be much more difficult if we waver—and likely even more terrifying. If I had stopped in the middle of that culvert, I am quite certain that terror would have taken over, making the culvert seem a lot smaller than it was. I am not sure how easy it would have been to retreat backwards into the darkness either. Maybe, for an instant, the darkness in the cave might have felt more comfortable—but not for long, as I would have been alone and the light from my cell phone would eventually have given out. If I wanted to get out of the darkness, I had to keep going.

It was clear that that also is the way life can be. Jesus told us that He is the light of the world—"I have come as a light to shine in this dark world, so that all who put their trust in me will no longer remain in the dark" (John 12:46). There is plenty of sadness and suffering around us that can invade my soul. I need to learn that there is a difference between focusing on the sadness around me and passing through it—not ignoring it, but being mindful to keep moving towards the light. We are called to bear one another's burdens, but there is a danger of being swallowed up by the burdens and finding ourselves trapped in the darkness. No matter how dark things get, I hope that I will always be able see some light and thereby remain hopeful.

The Breakfast Line

"You made all the delicate, inner parts of my body
and knit me together in my mother's womb.
Thank you for making me so wonderfully complex!
Your workmanship is marvelous—
how well I know it."– Psalm 139:13-14

It was a beautiful Thursday morning. The sun was shining, and there were no clouds in sight, the last ones having apparently blown away overnight. Most of us in our area have been mourning the lack of summer sunshine this year. It has become a standing joke in many conversations—and for good reason. So, this morning I had a smile on my face from the moment I opened my eyes and saw the sunshine. I laughed as I wrote, "Thank You, Father, for this day," in my journal. I used to write that quite often, and I still should, but I think I have neglected to do so on many occasions over the last several dreary months.

I looked out the window and saw three fledgling barn swallows sitting on the railing of our second floor deck. They were perched about eight feet from where I was standing, also facing the morning sun, spaced about one foot apart. They were obviously a family. I chuckled to myself as I watched them awkwardly trying to keep their balance on the slippery aluminum railing. No doubt they could fly or they would not have been there, but they appeared to be waiting for something.

You often see swallows lined up along a telephone line. It is what they seem to do, and I paid little attention to these three. Then I saw another swallow dart into view. It flew directly to the bird on the south end of the line and popped something into its mouth. Now I knew why this group was lined up. It was the breakfast line. Sure enough, in time the parent returned again with a little more breakfast for his or her young. (Apparently, the only way to distinguish between male and female barn swallows, without being invasive, is by the length of the tail—the male, of course, having a longer tail in order to attract females.)

I watched for a bit more and then returned to my desk to think about what I had just observed. I am a firm believer in the idea that God is constantly revealing His character and love. Sometimes I see it, and sometimes I don't, but His messages are constantly there to be received.

I started to wonder. At what point do these fledglings finally start to gather their own food? The parent, perhaps a fledgling last year, darts here and there, at times reaching speeds in excess of fifty kilometers per hour, skillfully catching hundreds of airborne insects. It is a finely honed art. But what about that moment in time when the young swallow has to learn to gather food on its own? Does it sit on the railing, waiting, and wondering what changed? That must be a moment of extreme tension. The fledgling calls out in desperation, feeling abandoned and forgotten—and yet the parent does not return to feed the child. The parent has apparently chosen to fly freely on its own. It is an extremely selfish act—or, at least, it must appear that way to the frightened young swallow.

Yet, the parent knows instinctively that something must change. The young must learn to snatch their own food out of the air or they will die. In order for the young swallows to become fully mature, in order for them to use what they have been given, in order for them to grow into everything they were intended to be, there must be that time of abandonment. It is a fearful time for them, to be sure, but nevertheless a necessary time. It is the only way they will learn the fine art of snatching bugs—preferably mosquitoes—from the air as they were intended to do.

So, I wonder—since I believe that God's loving ways are ever present—if there is something here for me this morning. I have gone through times of darkness, times of loneliness, times of fear—plenty of them. Perhaps I need to remember these young swallows on the railing. I, too, may have to accept a fearful feeling of abandonment, as God lovingly draws away, leading me to develop into the person He created me to be.

As I walked across our patio under the telephone line this morning, I noticed a streak of grayish white blobs on the ground. I looked up to see a family of swallows sitting in a row on the line—maybe not just waiting for breakfast.

Of Fire, Moths, and Mosquitoes

*"But Jesus often withdrew to lonely places
and prayed." – Luke 5:16 NIV*

*"He shrouded himself in darkness."
– Psalm 18:11*

*"Moths and all sorts of ugly creatures
hover about a lighted candle.
Can the candle help it?"
– Charles Dickens*

It was a warm Saturday summer evening, and Grace and I were sitting on the cottage chairs in our courtyard, waiting for "the kids" to come home. It was not the same kind of waiting as we had done years ago when the kids were teenagers. Our little grandson Adam was in our care for the evening, and we had decided to sit by the fire pit. We were enjoying our time together, listening to some music and watching as the stars pierced the night darkness. At one point, I turned to Grace and suggested that heaven will even be a lot better than this!

I wondered if the propane-fired flame would attract or repel the still lingering mosquitoes at this time of night. Then I noticed a white moth flying towards the flame and wondered how long his life would last. Surprisingly, he came very close to the flame, even landing on the lava rocks, before recognizing the danger and flying back into the darkness. I am quite sure that under normal circumstances this moth would have considered "staying in the light"—which could have led to his speedy demise. I know that moths prefer light at night and was quite surprised by his decision. Setting off into the darkness actually saved his life.

Once again, an everyday event stuck with me, and the quiet evening became my teacher. I think the darkness of loneliness is part of all of our lives. We are so afraid of being alone, especially being alone in the darkness and not knowing what is going on. And yet, can acceptance of "loneliness" also be life-saving for us? I was reminded of Jesus and His practice of seeking places of restorative loneliness. Perhaps that is something that is also necessary for us as we grow toward home.

By the way, we ended up putting on mosquito repellent—but it was still a beautiful evening.

Lessons from the Bathroom

*"Don't look out only for your own interests, but take
an interest in others, too." – Philippians 2:4*

*"Share each other's burdens, and in this way
obey the law of Christ." – Galatians 6:2*

When I was a child, there were five of us, including our parents, sharing one bathroom. Not that I can remember it very well, but that was just the way it was for most families.

I can still remember my Mom's parents not having running water and thus no modern toilet in their home. The options for relieving oneself were a framed wooden box in the basement (with a curtain that could be drawn in front of it and a pail underneath which needed regular cleaning), the outhouse about a hundred feet down a path from the door of the house, or the great outdoors. In winter, the outhouse path seemed a mile long, and the "toilet paper" (often a catalogue or a mandarin orange wrapper) felt very cold on an already frosty bottom. Sometimes we would crush a catalogue page in our hands to try to warm it and soften it while we conducted our business. Oddly, as far as I can remember, this was not really a major issue for me as a young boy—even though our home in the city had modern indoor plumbing. It never stood in my way of wanting to be on the farm.

I can also remember going to the well by the barn, pumping by hand to draw water into a bucket, and then carrying it back to the house. Bathing was conducted in a large galvanized tub in the middle of the kitchen floor. I have no idea where they kept that tub. I can just remember it sitting in the middle of the kitchen.

Water was scooped from a large pot steaming on the wood-fired stove nearby. Cool water would be added to temper it. I think we all used the same water—I can't remember for sure—but I have been told that that was the case. And there was one sink, a basin, that was used for washing both face and hands. No wonder I walked around dirty. When we brushed our teeth, I think we took a colored plastic tumbler from the cupboard, added a bit of water, and stepped outside. We dipped the toothbrush in the water to freshen it for more brushing and then rinsed with the same water. It was just the way it was.

Coming back to my childhood home, where five of us shared a bathroom, I can imagine that there were times when one of us became impatient waiting for a turn. I think we always waited until we were about to explode before even considering taking the time to go to the bathroom. Then we would prance around in front of the bathroom in the dark, pleading with the one inside to please hurry up. Depending on the state of that particular sibling relationship at the time, the one inside either mercifully hurried or deliberately took extra time. But one had to keep in mind that the tables could be turned the next day, and that worked to achieve civility most of the time.

I think that sort of realization could help the greater society even today, but, sadly, I don't think there are as many opportunities to learn it as there used to be. When I was young, we were forced to live close together and be mindful of each other. Sure, there were plenty of scraps, but there was also an awareness of each other's needs, which were much like our own.

The other day, Grace and I found ourselves hanging over the same small bathroom sink in the en suite bathroom that we have shared for more than twenty-eight years. We were going out, and both of us had to brush our teeth at the same time. We have developed a cooperative routine, taking turns. Sometimes a little frothy saliva falls on the other's hand, but no one gets upset. We just rinse it off, mumble an apology, and continue to brush. There is another sink in our home that no one normally uses, just down the hall. It is less than twenty feet from where we crowd around our sink, but we are accustomed to sharing this sink and are seemingly content with the arrangement.

In about a month's time, we will be moving—to a new addition we are building on this same home. Some in the family are calling it "the seniors' suite." The bathroom in our new master bedroom is much larger than our current one, which is probably fairly common by today's standards. It contains a tub, a separate walk-in shower, a little toilet "room," and a counter about seven feet long housing two basins. We will no longer have to share a sink when we brush our teeth. We will not have to accommodate the other because we will each have our own. Yes, I am looking forward to that, but there is an odd feeling of loss that I have become aware of. It is not the loss of sharing a sink that I am feeling, but a deeper loss, that has perhaps come along with our affluent society. I will love having my own sink to use when I please, but if that is all I had ever known, how would that have impacted my life? Perhaps we learn a lot by sharing a bathroom. It is the place that meets our basic needs, needs that we all have in common. When we share a bathroom, we are all aware of the fact that that it is needed by all and we cannot keep it for ourselves.

Our affluence has allowed us to "have our own" on many fronts. But has it made us less aware of others' needs and more focused on meeting our own needs? When I am at our cabin with our family, where we all still share one shower, I am mindful to shower when others are not wanting to, to have a quick shower to save water, and to leave the bathroom clean for the next user. Over the last few years, I have even gotten into the habit of taking a piece of paper towel in a public washroom and wiping around the sink that I have used before I leave. I am aware of how I would like the sink to be when I arrive, and I want to leave it that way for others. I wonder if those are lessons learned by sharing a bathroom at home.

Don't get me wrong. I am fine with having my own sink. I just wonder how long it will take until modern, enlightened design provides en suites with two toilets. Perhaps there are homes that already have a designated toilet for each occupant.

So, for the next month, Grace and I will continue to share the same sink while brushing our teeth—and then we won't. We will no longer have to make room for each other.

I stand, staring out the window and wondering how much of my life has been lived unaware of others. Do I assume that my needs will be met—or, worse, demand that my needs will be met by society—giving little attention to how fortunate I am? Can this perspective lead to an unhealthy insistence that my wants be met as well? And what is the cost of that pursuit to our grandchildren and to the greater good of society? How can I rather plant seeds of sharing and selflessness that will provide "fruit" for our grandchildren and others long after my own lifetime? That is what I would rather do—I hope.

Cookies and Sand Castles

*"The man wanted to justify his actions, so he
asked Jesus, 'And who is my neighbor?'
Jesus replied with a story." – Luke 10:29-30*

It was a Tuesday and a warm summer afternoon. I was sitting in
my office, working on preparations for a staff retreat, when I had
a sudden craving for a cookie. This was not the first time. My love
of cookies might be one of the reasons we serve cookies every
afternoon at Hallmark, the retirement community where I work.
Another reason might be that everyone else in the community
also likes afternoon cookies!

There is an East Indian bakery and pizza shop in the strip mall
next to us that we periodically visit in order to purchase a piece of
pizza or some cookies. This afternoon, I was after a cookie.

When I stepped out of the building, I was surprised by the
afternoon heat—it was around 30 degrees Celsius (close to
90 degrees Fahrenheit) again. We are going to remember this
summer for a long time. I stayed in the shade as much as possible
as I walked past the other shops offering produce, meat, and other
goods and turned into the bakery.

As I was entering, an elderly Muslim man was walking towards
me to exit the store. We smiled at each other as we passed. As
I approached the counter, the store owner, a Sikh, recognized
me immediately. He pressed his palms together and bowed his
cordial greeting. I returned it to him as I always do. I commented
on the increase in his stock and gathered up a small container of
cookies—which is what I thought I had come for.

At the counter, the merchant told me that the man I had just passed was a very religious Muslim man. He then went on to relate a story that the Muslim had told him. The merchant and I often talk about our respective faiths quite openly, and so I expected that this brief encounter would be another normal conversation.

This is how the story went. Once upon a time (and the Muslim man claimed that this is a true story that can be found in history books), a king and queen in Saudi Arabia were walking along a sandy beach. They came upon a man building a structure out of sand. The queen asked what he was building. He replied that he was building a castle and asked her if she would like to buy it. She asked him how much. He responded, "One dollar" (or whatever the basic unit of currency was in that time). She pulled out the required coin and passed it to him. The king and queen walked on, with the king feeling somewhat perplexed.

That night, the king had a troubling dream in which he came across a huge, glorious castle bearing the name of his wife. Of course, he was all set to enter when he was refused entry by two security guards. This shocked him, so he explained that the person whose name was on the castle was his wife. They answered, "Maybe on earth but not here!"

When he awoke, the king was quite troubled. He got up early and walked back down the beach to see if he could find the same man again. Sure enough, there he was, building another structure. The king asked the man what it was, and the man gave the same answer as before: "It is a castle." The king asked if he could buy the castle. The man agreed to the sale, but when the king asked how much, the amount was greater than all the wealth that the king had. The king was quite upset. Recalling the price of the other castle from the previous day, he demanded an explanation as to why the price had changed so drastically. The response from the castle builder was: "The queen bought the castle without seeing it completed. You saw it completed, and now you want to buy it."

It is quite a profound story. The moral, according to my Sikh friend, was that we all should have faith in God without demanding to know the outcome. That is up to Him.

I think that story might be why I had a craving for a cookie this afternoon.

By the way, the religious Muslim man comes every day to pick up "leftovers" from that shop and feed them to birds. He is apparently the birdman of Abbotsford.

As I left, I was given another valuable nugget, unsolicited. My Sikh friend asked if I knew why Sikh men grow long beards. I did not. Apparently, one of the Sikh gurus was asked the same question centuries ago. He responded: "When God returns, if I do not have a long beard, what will I wash His feet with?"

And so I enjoyed a good afternoon treat—and the cookie was good too.

Tie Rods and God

*"It is better to trust in the LORD than to put
confidence in man." – Psalm 118:8 KJV*

What was to be a routine visit to the local garbage dump (or
"community center") turned out to be much more.

We were at our place called Forest Dreams in the Cariboo region
and took a drive to the dump with a couple of bags of household
refuse. There is little opportunity to recycle in this region, other
than the basic separation of metals, wood, and construction
materials. Everything else gets tossed into a crevice dug into the
earth and is stirred around weekly by a tractor. There is also a little
"share shed" at every dump in the Cariboo region, where people
leave anything that they think might be useful to someone else. It
is a great idea, and it serves a very practical recycling purpose. We
ourselves have come away with many great treasures—and even
done some early Christmas "shopping" there!

The ten-kilometer drive from our home to the dump was
leisurely. We turned off the highway and bumped along the
washboard road to the dump. I dropped Grace off to do some
shopping at the share shed and proceeded to the trench to toss in
the trash.

As I put my Dodge Ram 3500 four-wheel-drive Cummins
diesel into drive and accelerated, I sensed something was wrong.
Just seconds before, everything had been fine. I went another fifty
meters before I realized that I had absolutely no steering at all.
How could that be possible? We had just come off a highway less
than a minute earlier where we had been driving at over ninety
kilometers per hour!

I had no idea what had happened, but I knew that I wasn't going to go any further. With the truck safely in park, I climbed out and peered into the shadows under the front end of my truck. To my surprise, I saw a steering control arm dangling uselessly. I was shocked. I had never had anything like this happen before. This truck was "built to last" and was quite new, with only one hundred and twenty-five thousand kilometers on it. I had had it serviced just three months earlier. I followed the control arm to where it had broken away from the front left wheel. I shuddered as I thought of what could have happened if it had broken loose when we were driving at high speed. I whispered a prayer of thanks to God for sparing us.

What followed was a wonderful experience of being cared for by the many local folks at the dump. It truly functioned as a community center that day. We were in need, and that seemed to be all that mattered to these people. We were touched again and again, as everything we needed was provided in a gentle way. Before noon the next day, my truck had been repaired and was back on the road.

I have thought a lot about that incident, which could have had a much different outcome. The part that broke is about the size of a spark plug (or a garlic, for those who relate to food better). It had sheared off completely. We lost all ability to steer the truck because of a tiny part worth less than a hundred dollars, about point four percent of the value of the vehicle. We could have been stranded on a dark and stormy winter night, we could have careened off the road, or we could have lost control and plowed into another vehicle. I have read stories on the Internet of similar malfunctions that did not end nearly as well as ours did.

Perhaps this connects with my life to some degree. I often think that I am in control—the steering wheel is firmly in my grip, and it appears that my life is responding to my direction. Then something unexpected happens, and I lose all control. This can happen quickly, without any warning.

And it can be the little things that are often overlooked and yet play a critical role in my life that break down—little things such as sleeping well, eating what I should, and listening to God's voice in the many forms it takes. If any of these is sheared off, the "tie rod" of my life will give way. Maybe, in a weird way, God can be seen as that tie rod. I think I am steering, and my life seems to be going where I direct it, but if that tie rod is not in place, I am not going anywhere. It is God who brings His will and His love into my world and keeps me safe and on the right road. If I want to arrive home safely, He will have to stay connected and direct my life.

Time Together

"For each day he carries us in his arms."
– Psalm 68:19

Last night, I held Ben, our newest grandson, in my arms for about half an hour. He is just two weeks old, and that is the longest period of time we have spent with each other since he was born. I watched as his fragile, little body expanded and contracted with each breath, assuring me that he was still living and present with us. I was reminded of the amazing gift of life that has been given to all of us.

I prayed for Ben as he lay peacefully against my chest, fully trusting me. What else could he do? He is totally dependent, and there is nothing he can do but lie there and relish his new life. Yes, he complains when discomfort comes his way—he has no control over that either. He hasn't learned to hide his pain or pretend that he is in pain when he isn't. He is what he is.

I wondered what life would be like for him in our ever-struggling world. New life constantly arrives, bringing hope and joy. And old life appears to leave, causing sorrow so deep at times that we fear we will break or collapse under the load. A time will come when all of that pain will be a thing of the past, but deep pain had yet to come to Ben. Still, I knew it would. It comes to all of us who live for long.

For now, Ben lay peacefully and contentedly in my arms, and I allowed his contentment to touch me. I turned my chair to face the beauty outside the windows—evidence of God's sustaining love for us and His abiding presence with us. I felt Ben's warm body and his fine hair that tickled my nose, and I was so grateful for Ben. He was new to our family—but not to God's!

Abscission

"There is a time for everything,
and a season for every activity under the heavens:
a time to be born and a time to die."
– Ecclesiastes 3:10-2 NIV

"Teach us to number our days." – Psalm 90:12 NIV

It has been the most beautiful summer I have ever known here in the Fraser Valley. If you love sunshine from dawn to dusk, no mosquitoes, and warm evenings and mornings, this will be the summer to remember for a long time. Yes, we had some pretty oppressive heat that caused many to scramble to buy air conditioners—they were being snapped up like Canucks hockey tickets during a winning season. The unusually cold summer in eastern Canada provided a surplus of A/C units to meet the intense demand around here. We bought two for our own home and were delighted with the difference they made.

I have loved this summer. But, as I write this in the first week of September, rain is pouring down. We have had a wet and sometimes stormy few days, leaving over 500,000 BC Hydro customers without power, for over two full days in many cases. Summer already seems like a distant memory. How ridiculous is that?

Apparently, we had as much rain in one day over the last weekend as we had had in the previous four months combined—a lot of rain for this dry land. The signs of drought have been everywhere. Watering gardens and lawns, when permitted, could only be done at certain times. The mature trees around us were left on their own, and their survival was not guaranteed.

The photo with this chapter is of a hazelnut tree beside our home. It is representative of various other trees on our property. In the photo, it can clearly be seen that the tree has mysteriously cut off the flow of nourishment to certain leaves. This will reduce the amount of water needed by the tree and allow the tree itself to survive. I have no idea how the tree decides which leaves get cut off and left to die in order to save the whole. What is very clear is that the struggle for survival this summer has caused selective purging. I learned that this natural process is called abscission.

I often think that God uses His creation to teach us—if we are willing to spend some time listening and reflecting. Sobering thoughts came to me as I wondered if abscission is also what happens with humanity on some level. In order for the community to survive, does the community decide that "someone" has to go? As I age, I wonder if I would be willing to accept the idea that I need to move aside, without protest, for the benefit of the greater community. The dying leaves hanging precariously on the tree have taken on new meaning for me. In that state, they do not last long. The slightest breeze causes them to flutter to the ground, and in just a few days they will disappear, their presence not even missed.

This may seem like morbid thinking, but could it be freeing as well? It is the way of life and death—and I am assured that love is stronger than death. In that I place my hope.

No Longer Running—at Least, Not as Fast

*"Even so, I have noticed one thing, at least, that is good.
It is good for people to eat, drink, and enjoy their work
under the sun during the short life God has given them, and
to accept their lot in life. And it is a good thing to receive
wealth from God and the good health to enjoy it. To enjoy
your work and accept your lot in life—this is indeed a gift
from God. God keeps such people so busy enjoying life
that they take no time to brood over the past."
– Ecclesiastes 5:18-20*

*"A man is not old until his regrets take the
place of dreams." – John Barrymore*

I now have watched four grandchildren learn to run. And, in most cases, I have watched them learn to walk too.

Earlier, I had watched our three sons learn to walk and eventually run, but it is different now. You see, when our sons learned to walk and run, I could be the "role model" of sorts. I could outwalk and outrun them for years. When they learned to run, Dad was still pretty fast on his feet. There was no such thing as running away from me—unless I allowed them to do so. I remember pretending to chase them at breakneck speed as they outdistanced me, knowing full well that I could very quickly make up the ground between us at any time. I quite enjoyed watching our sons learn to run.

But, a year ago, I was beaten in a footrace by Asia, our oldest granddaughter. She was maybe ten. I am convinced that she was quite fast for a ten-year-old, but that was of little consolation. I refused to believe it. We had another footrace this past summer so that I could prove my fleet-footedness. That was a mistake. The emotional trauma of losing again was eclipsed by the stiffness in my legs two days later. I may not try to prove my superior speed to her again. It is unlikely that I will pick up speed over the next year—or ever, for that matter.

That is the point of my thoughts today. I now am watching our two-year-old grandson Adam, who seems to enjoy running all over the place. I don't think he gives it a second thought. He will run back and forth in the room, gesturing with his pointing finger, showing us where he is going and inviting us to join him. I should get all my footraces with him in very soon, and perhaps my reputation of being faster than he is will last longer than the reality.

Adam is moving into his potential. We cheer when he tries to pronounce new words. We "listen" intently as he uses his gestures to tell us what happened moments or days ago. His recall is so fresh, the retelling flows freely. Just don't ask me what I did yesterday. If I could still run, I would run and get my journal in the hope that it might trigger my memory. More likely, I will just hope I am not asked about yesterday in too much detail.

I am reading a book called *Being Mortal*. Do I really need the reminder? It is not that I was unaware of my mortality, but I was quite satisfied to believe that "downhill" was up ahead somewhere, at least a decade or more away. I am only 62. But the book tells me that we generally peak around age 30 and by 40 the downhill movement is well underway. Our body starts to wear out long before we are aware of it. By age 60, the retinas of our eyes receive only about 30 percent of the light that they were open to when we were children. Forty percent of us will develop textbook dementia—whatever that is—by age 85. There is more, but I can't recall it just now.

I have to come to grips with the fact that, no matter how hard I may try, even if I started training to run marathons (there is not even the remotest possibility of that!), parts of my body are destined to wear out. No, they are wearing out, day by day. Yes, I may "improve" a part of me with committed exercise, but I have no chance of reversing the general direction. And I have to accept that fact. Fortunately, I have lots of company, since I am part of the aging baby boomer tsunami.

But there is a surprising contentment, an inner peace, that seems to be growing somewhere inside me. At times, I wonder about that. Is contentment a good thing? Am I in danger of floating along towards my departure from this world? Or is this contentment allowing me—no, calling me—to reflect more deeply on the fact that I am loved and to trust more deeply that God, in His unfathomable love, will bring me home?

I still have lots of dreams—not of running marathons, and maybe not of beating the grandkids in a footrace—but I have dreams. I suppose there are some regrets too, but they have to be dug up for me to find them more often than not—and for the most part I don't want to. The dreams are still there regularly. Maybe more to the point, dreaming and reflecting go hand in hand. I love to sit with a cup of coffee in the early morning and soak up God's love. I think of family and friends and wonder if I am helping to leave this world a better place. I hope so.

I am not in a rush to leave this world. There is so much to be thankful for and so much life I feel I still have to live—but that doesn't necessarily include winning a footrace with my grandchildren!

"Grandpa, Can You Please Stay for a Few More Weeks?"

"Jesus called a little child to him and put the child among them." – Matthew 18:2

It was our last day at Forest Dreams, after we had spent four weeks at our beautiful place in the Cariboo. I cannot come up with a way to describe the time there. One of the words would be "busy," and another would be "wonderful." I am so grateful for the opportunity we have had to spend a lot of time with our three grandkids, who live only half an hour's drive away. They are two, four, and six years of age and love spending time at Forest Dreams. We all do.

Our eldest son Ryan had come over with Ethan, his four-year-old, to pick up their quads and various other items, including shoes, life jackets, and flotation devices—evidence of adventures that were now memories. If possible, I had tried to record each day up here in a journal. I once read that journaling can help convince you that you really did live an event. Maybe that is one of the reasons for my addiction to journaling.

After I had helped Ryan load up their stuff, we were having a cup of coffee on the Adirondack chairs in the warm afternoon sun. I had given Ethan a root beer. He rotated the can in his hand and said, "It looks like 'A' and 'W.'"

Laughingly, I responded: "Yes, and you are learning to read." Or maybe not. In a community where one has a choice of Tim Horton's, Dairy Queen, Subway, or A and W for fast food, brand recognition is a given. But lately he has shown a keen interest in reading.

There were mixed feelings on this last day at Forest Dreams, as Grace, Ryan, Ethan, and I cherished the time we had had together, knowing that tomorrow would be different. We did not talk about tomorrow but rather of the wonderful time we had spent together over the last several weeks.

When Grace and Ryan appeared to be engaged in their own conversation, Ethan came up to me, his orange cap tilted back on his head. With his big, blue eyes looking directly into mine, he said: "Grandpa, can you please stay for a few more weeks?"

How do you answer that? A stroke of genius came to me. "Go and ask Grandma about that."

I don't think he did, but at least I didn't have to provide an answer. We had planned on returning home the next day, but for an instant I considered staying for a few more weeks.

Why would I even consider it? Much had to be done at home. The responsibilities of daily living were calling us, and we were aware that others at home had been performing extra duties so that we could spend the time away. Was I crazy? Probably, but I still carry that line around with me and my irresponsible fleeting thought that maybe I could stay for a few more weeks.

Grandkids aren't perfect. Over the last four weeks, rarely had we gotten through a meal without at least one spill. Tiredness from a full day had resulted in some whining, especially at mealtimes. The grandkids were highly skilled at mind control and manipulation. The youngest, two-year-old Myra, would spill yet another glass of water, or perhaps even dump her fully loaded plate onto the floor and then look up at us with large, endearing eyes and a wonderful ear-to-ear grin. It would leave us speechless.

All that aside, and as tired as I was, I seriously wanted to stay for a few more weeks with the grandkids. They had challenged us every day, in a good way, and had seemed to have no end of energy and ideas. Grace and I would drag ourselves into bed at the end of another day, clearly understanding why we had had our own kids when we were young. And our other two sons had not yet started to have children. We shuddered to think of having to maintain this pace for another ten years.

I am in love with our grandchildren. I am not unaware of their imperfections. I wish that they were as perfect as I was at their age, but they are their father's children (and their mother's), and we should not expect anything different. But I am in love with them. On top of that, I like them.

Did I get a little taste of God's love for us when I had that momentary lapse and considered staying for a few more weeks? I am so imperfect, so challenging. Perhaps at my age and with my vast experience, I do not have the courage to look to my heavenly Father and ask Him to "stay for a few more weeks." After all, He has so much to do, and I am such a goof. Maybe I am too proud to ask Him to spend time with me.

In Matthew 18, Jesus' disciples asked, "Who is the greatest in the Kingdom of Heaven?" Jesus put a little child in His lap and answered, "Anyone who becomes as humble as this little child is the greatest in the Kingdom of Heaven."

When Ethan looked at me and asked me to stay longer, he did so in complete humility. He never considered whether he was worthy of my time. All that was important to him was that he loved me and wanted me to stay for a few more weeks. For that moment, that was enough reason for me. Ethan knew that he was loved by me. He had no thought of having to earn or deserve our time—he just loved Grace and me.

I love savoring that question from Ethan. It gives me a little glimpse of God's love for me. It reminds me that He wants to spend time with me simply because He loves me.

Biblical Land Transaction

*"So be truly glad. There is a wonderful joy ahead,
even though you must endure many trials
for a little while." – 1 Peter 1:8*

I read a very interesting chapter in the book of Jeremiah this morning, chapter 32. I was looking for a prophecy that was quoted in Matthew and found an unexpected treasure hidden in the story of Jeremiah.

The authorship of the book of Jeremiah is usually attributed to Jeremiah and/or his followers. He has been nicknamed the "weeping prophet" because he prophesied about the impending destruction of Jerusalem. The people of Israel—God's chosen ones—had turned from God and succumbed to evil practices, and God had had enough. The destruction was going to happen. This was obviously not a popular message.

One of the kings of Judah during that time was Zedekiah. He imprisoned Jeremiah for constantly repeating that Jerusalem would fall to the Babylonians and that Zedekiah himself would be taken in chains to Babylon. Jeremiah warned Zedekiah, "If you fight against the Babylonians, you will never succeed" (Jeremiah 32:5). King Zedekiah did not want this hopeless message to dominate the news, and he decided that his best option was to imprison Jeremiah, in the hope of silencing him.

While in prison, Jeremiah received a further message. His cousin Hanamel came to visit him and pleaded with him to buy his field. Maybe he believed Jeremiah's prophecy and felt that this was his only way of getting any value out of his land before the Babylonians took it over.

Obviously, Jeremiah believed the prophecy about the coming destruction of Jerusalem given to him by God. One would think that he might have reminded his cousin of this and questioned why he was offering him his property, knowing full well that it would be lost to the Babylonians. It would be a pretty poor investment, to say the least. He might have been justified in questioning his cousin's motives

Instead, the story tells us that Jeremiah realized that "the message...was from the LORD" (verse 8). Jeremiah paid his cousin seventeen pieces of silver for the land. The transaction was fully documented with a sealed deed and an unsealed copy, carefully preserved for future reference.

The transaction was conducted in front of many witnesses, including "all the men of Judah who were there in the courtyard of the guardhouse" (verse 12). Surely these witnesses must have been confused. The guy, who had been constantly repeating the message about the takeover of Jerusalem and its surrounding area had just bought a piece of land. Either he was incredibly dumb, or he knew something that they did not know. Or maybe he was just giving out his prophecy to scare people into selling their land to him at a bargain price.

Jeremiah cleared the confusion up pretty quickly: "This is what the LORD of Heaven's Armies, the God of Israel says: 'Take both this sealed deed and the unsealed copy, and put them into a pottery jar to preserve them for a long time.' For this is what the LORD of Heaven's Armies, the God of Israel, says: 'Someday people will again own property here in this land and will buy and sell houses and vineyards and fields'" (32:14-15). Jeremiah was certainly not backing off from his prophecy of impending destruction—but he was now also holding out the faint hope that "someday" there would be a restoration.

Jeremiah then prayed a very powerful prayer in the presence of the witnesses, outlining Israel's unfaithfulness and the inevitability of Jerusalem's destruction. He finished off with the contradictory statement: "And yet, O Sovereign LORD, you have told me to buy the field—paying good money for it before these witnesses—even though the city will soon be handed over to the

Babylonians" (32:25). It appears that Jeremiah may have been confused as well. What God had asked him to do made no sense to him based on the message that he had been giving over and over again. But he trusted God enough to do it anyway. His action was meant to be a powerful message about God's faithfulness to His promises: "For someday I will restore prosperity to them. I, the LORD, have spoken!" (32:44)

There is much that I do not understand about my life, and about life in general. Things happen in my life, and in others' lives, that defy my need to comprehend. And yet, I must trust that, someday, our loving Father will restore all. Perhaps the most perplexing events may actually have great meaning if I will pay attention and listen rather than being consumed by them.

Jesus told His followers: "Don't let your hearts be troubled. Trust in God, and trust also in me. There is more than enough room in my Father's house. If this were not so, would I have told you that I am going to prepare a place for you? When everything is ready, I will come and get you, so that you will always be with me where I am" (John 14:1-3).

At times, that may seem like a long way off, and it is. Bad things happen, but perhaps we can see that behind them, as in the case of Jeremiah's land transaction, there is a promise of a very beautiful "home" awaiting us. That promise will be fulfilled. And perhaps then we can accept what confuses us and appears to defy any explanation. The things most confusing may be indicators, too, of what is to come. Maybe the story of imminent trouble and a distant promise is the story of our lives every day. I hope that if I listen, trusting in God and His love, I may see at least some of the larger picture unfolding. If not, I hope that I will be able to trust God like Jeremiah did, even when it doesn't seem to make sense.

Of Mushrooms and Life

"We now have this light shining in our hearts, but we ourselves are like fragile clay jars containing this great treasure. This makes it clear that our great power is from God, not from ourselves. We are pressed on every side with troubles, but we are not crushed. We are perplexed but not driven to despair. We are hunted down, but never abandoned by God. We get knocked down, but we are not destroyed." – 2 Corinthians 4:7-9

"Tomorrow we go for a long walk, no matter what."

These were Grace's words just before bedtime Saturday night. A statement like that is best left alone, because any response on my part could be misunderstood. We had just been up in the Cariboo for a month, and the eats had been very good and plenteous. Now we were back home, with the discipline of urban life haunting us on day two of our return. I was fine with the idea of getting some exercise as well, but I wondered if the commitment might wane if the predicted rain for the morning materialized.

Well, the predicted rain did arrive right on time for our long walk. Grace was donning her waterproof clothing consistent with her resolve for a long walk this morning. I was fine with the idea—after all, who would want to stay inside and read while cradling a cup of warm coffee when one could be walking in torrential rain?

As we started out on our walk, we noticed many mushrooms pushing their way up through the earth. The conditions of late—plenty of rain and warmth—were ideal for rapid mushroom growth. No wonder someone had come up with the idea of using "mushroom" as a verb to describe extremely rapid growth. A mushroom that becomes

visible to the eye is the fruiting body of a colony of underground mycelia, or roots, that may actually be centuries old. Under the right conditions, a mushroom bud forms. This bud consists of tons of preformed cells. When there is plenty of rainfall, the mycelium pulls water into the mushroom bud and literally uses hydraulic pressure to force the cap of the mushroom bud up through the earth overnight.

When we had been in the Cariboo earlier in the week, we had seen this amazing phenomenon all around us. Mushroom caps had sprouted up several inches, at times still covered with the humus that had provided the bed for their growth.

On our morning walk at home, I noticed a peculiar sight that caused me to reflect on it throughout the day. We had crossed the railway tracks into a denser part of the forest and noticed many mushrooms bordering the trail. Two mushrooms, likely from the same mycelium, were growing side by side. The caps were quite different in shape, but not appearance. You see, one had grown without any apparent barrier, but the other had grown up under the weight of a branch that had forced the mushroom cap to fold around it, disfiguring the cap. One mushroom did not have to lift a tree branch to develop into its potential. The other did.

There seems to be so much in God's natural order that can teach me. These two fragile little mushrooms grew side by side and from the same colony. One had a tremendous load to bear in order to blossom, while the other apparently faced no challenges at all. They could not choose. They could only grow where they were.

People who collect and consume mushrooms are called mycophagists. If they were picking them for the market, I assume that mycophagists would pass by the deformed mushroom as imperfect and thus inferior. Yet it had a much harder life than its more perfect-looking neighbor.

Grace and I returned later in the day to capture a photo of this lesson.

Life is not fair. Perhaps that is one of the most important lessons for us all to learn—not so that we can muster up pity for ourselves, but rather so that we can be grateful for life itself. We all grow up from the common "mycelium" of the human race. We are born with no choice, but as we grow, our choices influence the way we live. Some of us are born "free" and some "under a branch." I doubt that any of us will get through our normal span of years here on earth without feeling a weight of some kind.

One of the wonderful components of the Christian life is that, whether we live believing it or not, God is with us in all things. He knows what we carry and has promised never to give us more than we can bear. Life comes from Him—and He lives within us.

Spiders and Mushrooms

"God has given you one face, and you make yourself another." – William Shakespeare

"We are so accustomed to disguise ourselves to others that in the end we become disguised to ourselves." – François Duc de La Rochefoucauld

Someone flipped a switch when I wasn't looking, and fall arrived. We had been experiencing perhaps the nicest summer in the last twenty years in southern British Columbia, but that unbroken run of glorious sunshine has come to an abrupt end. This was a memorable summer, but it is behind us now. The cold fall rains have begun. Yes, we will likely have a few more days of sun, but the earth will inexorably cool in the chill of the night, as the sun begins its annual retreat. We will lose about four minutes of daylight per day from now until December 21, which adds up to about eight hours less daylight than we had in mid-summer by the time Christmas arrives. We have survived this darkening of our world in the past, and we will survive again. But I am grateful that the sun eventually gets tired of where it winters each year and comes back again in the spring. (That is obviously not the correct scientific explanation, but it will do for me.)

This time of year seems to bring out the spiders. Or perhaps it is just that by now they have grown big enough to make their presence much more obvious. And with the presence of spiders come spider webs. On our morning walks, we encounter dew-soaked webs spanning the trail, draping across our faces, and leaving a wet, cold line. This often causes us to step back as if we weren't powerful enough to break through their delicate threads. Spider webs adorn the fence posts, clinging to the barbed wire, and cloak the bushes—all much more visible because of the morning dew.

A couple of days ago, I came across a remarkable web, elaborately spun between some branches and a deck post. The dew highlighted it, and the morning sun added an artistic beauty. I did not see the spider anywhere, nor any unfortunate insect snared among the weavings. Still, I had no doubt that a spider was waiting close by, watching for a trembling of the web that would alert him to the fact that breakfast was ready.

A thought occurred to me. This spider, along with thousands of others, had spun a magnificent web overnight. There had been no audience to cheer him on—other than perhaps his Creator. If the spider and I could have had a conversation, I would have liked to have asked him why he made this web with such intricate beauty when it was likely that no one would ever notice it. I imagine he might have responded by saying: "Because it is what I do, it is what I am meant to do—and it provides a pretty good meal to boot."

Along the trail a little later, we came across a fairly substantial mushroom that we had not seen the morning before. This is the time of year that mushrooms appear to push their way up through the earth overnight. I have no idea how something that delicate can make its way through the matted humus, but it does. The forest is full of amazing mushrooms, majestic fungi. They, too, just do what they were meant to do, what they were made to do, without any fanfare. No audience of the forest cheers them on. They have enough inside themselves to become what they were meant to become.

No one told the spider or the mushroom that what they were made to do was not good enough and that they should perhaps be something different. In fact, no one told them one way or the other what to do. They just did it.

Even the simplest forms of life can teach me so much. Is it possible that as humans we, too, can connect with what our Creator planted in us and bring it to life without need of an audience? That may sound ridiculous and idealistic, but is it wrong to think that it is possible? If I am prepared to believe that it is possible for myself, can I also learn to treat others with the same respect, believing in their beauty and gift?

And maybe we do have an audience—an audience of One, who loves us dearly and cheers us on as He sees the beauty He planted in us come alive.

I Believe in Meadows

"These are the proverbs...Their purpose is to teach people wisdom and discipline, to help them understand the insights of the wise. Their purpose is to teach people to live disciplined and successful lives, to help them do what is right, just, and fair." – Proverbs 1:1-3

I awoke shortly after 7:00 a.m., got up, and walked over to the living room window. I smiled as I looked out over the still sleeping city, wondering at the quietness that can exist in this concrete and steel jungle stretching ever upward. Maybe the penthouse suites are most expensive because they are closest to heaven—people are willing to pay a lot to gain separation from the earth.

Our condominium is on the third floor, close enough to the ground to be convenient and yet high enough to offer a beautiful view of downtown Vancouver. A few years ago, one could see distinct buildings across Burrard Inlet from our place. Today, other than the tallest, the buildings all seem to blend together as an indistinct mass—a porridge of structures.

I took a picture of the morning sun casting a pinkish glow on the buildings surrounding us, with the city of Vancouver in the background. I turned around for a moment, and when I looked back to view the city some more, there was nothing to be seen. The mass of structures housing hundreds of thousands of people, making Vancouver the most densely populated city in Canada, was completely invisible. In the few seconds that I had turned away, the city had vanished completely, lost behind a dense fog bank that had rolled in from the ocean. If I had arrived at that moment and was new on the scene, I might have told others that there was nothing beyond where we lived, at least nothing that I could see. Having been here before, I was intrigued and stood there in anticipation, waiting for the city to reappear—as it did a few moments later. It was spectacular as it loomed up gray and mysterious, barely visible through the fog, but still unmistakable. As the fog gradually lifted, the city's outlines hardened and sharpened, and it once again took up its normal place on the horizon.

Ah, the elderly among us. They have seen "the city" come and go and return again. Every day we are reminded of the perilous times that we are in. Our infrastructures, moral, economic, political, and social, often built with care at some time in the past, seem to be decaying at an alarming rate. Inertia from an unknown source seems to be pulling us out of control and pushing us inexorably toward a cataclysmic demise. We may have a good idea of what is at the heart of this decline, but we either do not know what to do about it or are unwilling to take the risk of getting involved. Rather than tackling the problem head on, we may just be hoping that those we love will not be affected by it. Of course, that is naïve, but to speak our thoughts out loud can be frightening. What happens if the language of the day is not our own? What happens if we are wrong? What happens if we cannot find a safe way to express our concerns without facing ridicule and misunderstanding?

A walk this morning took us by a corner bench where three disheveled people were engaged in a deep and very vocal conversation. Their language was offensive and belligerent, making all passersby nervous and anxious not to be noticed by these unstable people. I looked down or away as if not to acknowledge their presence at all—ridiculous really, but how else could I escape?

I entered the shelter of the local grocery store while Grace stayed outside with the dog. A moment later, two of the three were in the store, just as vocal and disruptive. I felt very sorry for the staff member who tried to calm them, without success. They affected everyone near them. We knew they were not well, of course, but they affected us all. I believe most of us there would love to have helped them, but we did not know how. Or were we just being selfish, focused on protecting ourselves, because to be in their presence was frightening?

Where is the fog when we need it? If only it would roll in again and block out the view of this chaos so that we could pretend that it does not exist. If someone could just step up and lend more money to delay the bankruptcy, perhaps that could be the solution. Or maybe someone could offer to shelter these people somewhere, anywhere, as long as it was far away from us.

Who are our guides during this time? Who is giving direction? Who is trying to speak as an authority during this time?

What would happen if a group of elderly citizens in our community were sought out and asked to share their thoughts with us? Maybe it would help if we would listen to them instead of feeling the need to correct them and pass them by as being irrelevant. Perhaps there are "proverbs of the people," accumulated nuggets of wisdom from our elders, that can guide us.

But what if we are not prepared to consider that "manual," not prepared to listen to that group of people, who might prove to be a valuable resource? How much is lost if we refuse to listen to traditional wisdom? Without that help, how will we ever find our way out of the jungle? Maybe we never will while on this earth. But I believe that there are meadows, open places full of sunshine and warmth in the midst of the jungle, that we can find—and perhaps even the bush is not all that bad either.

When Will I See the Light Better?

"Then God said, 'Let lights appear in the sky to separate the day from the night. Let them be signs to mark the seasons, days, and years. Let these lights in the sky shine down on the earth.'" – Genesis 1:14

"If you carefully obey the commands I am giving you today, and if you love the LORD your God and serve him with all your heart and soul, then he will send the rains in their proper seasons— the early and late rains—so you can bring in your harvests of grain, new wine, and olive oil." – Deuteronomy 11:14

This morning, I slept in a bit. At this time of year, it is usually dark when I have my morning cup of coffee in the library, but this morning dawn was arriving when I climbed out of bed. It was a still fall morning, with lots of fallen leaves on the yard. I turned the coffee machine on, and while I was waiting for the warming cycle to complete, I looked around a bit. I was struck by the beauty of the early dawn. I decided to sit on our couch in

the great room, with the lights off and the fireplace on, enjoy my coffee, and gather in the beauty. There are many in our life to pray for, which I did as I sat in silence.

I noticed, at least I thought I did, a light from a cell tower up on Lower Sumas Mountain. It was among the leaves still clinging to a birch tree that was partly obscuring my view of the mountain. I knew the cell tower was there, but the light seemed to disappear as quickly as I had noticed it. I wondered if perhaps what I had seen was a plane preparing to land at our local airport, but I could not seem to locate it again. It would be on a very low approach if it were a plane, and so I considered going outside to watch it. But there again was the light—it was the cell tower. If I held my head in the "perfect" place, I could see the flashing light. But if I made the slightest movement, the light was completely blocked again.

A thought came to me. I realized that, in a few days, fall would force all the leaves from the tree and then the light would always be visible. By winter, it would be easily seen. I wondered, when I am in the "fall" of my life here on earth, will this provide me with an opportunity to see more of God's light and love? Is it possible that as more is stripped away, I will actually be able to see more clearly?

The leaves were necessary to nourish the tree, but they will not be present for a season, even though life for the tree goes on. Their absence will allow me to see the light whenever I look for it. Maybe the fall of my life will allow me to see God's ever present love and light with greater ease. That is something to look forward to. I do love fall.

A Rock and a Cross

"All of them ate the same spiritual food, and all of them drank the same spiritual water. For they drank from the spiritual rock that traveled with them, and that rock was Christ." – 1 Corinthians 10:3-4

It was a typical overcast morning with all of the usual components—coffee, reflection, reading, and writing. Then I donned my plastic Lee Valley garden shoes and my heavy flannel shirt, and Grace and I stepped outside to start our morning walk.

As we crossed over a portion of the lawn on the way to the trail, Grace paused and bent over, beckoning me. "Look at this!"

I retraced my steps, crouched beside her, and noticed that the relentless rains had exposed something quite amazing—the top of a rock, with a distinct dark brown cross centered on the exposed light gray surface. We dug the rock out as a keepsake.

I have thought long and hard about that cross. To us, the cross represents the death of Jesus, an unfathomable sacrifice of love, a sacrifice that was necessary to allow us to be reinstated as children of

God. And where did that cross show up this morning? In the midst of the dirt, likely trodden on by us many times and driven over by quads. That is where Jesus often seems to show up—in the mess of life, in suffering, sadness, sickness, and confusion.

We go through times when we seem to be surrounded by a lot of suffering and challenge. I know that these things are always present, but at these times their intensity seems much more pronounced. The image of the cross on the rock, almost hidden by the dirt, will stay with me. It will serve as reassurance that Jesus is always present, no matter what the circumstance. It is not a matter of how I feel, but a matter of His promise to us in Matthew 28:20: "And be sure of this: I am with you always, even to the end of the age."

That rock is now sitting on our kitchen windowsill—as a reminder.

I Will Carry You

"I was thrust into your arms at my birth.
You have been my God from the moment
I was born." – Psalm 22:10

"For he will order his angels
to protect you wherever you go.
They will hold you up with their hands
so you won't even hurt your foot
on a stone."– Psalm 91:11-12

I came home a little earlier on a beautiful fall afternoon to go for a walk with Grace. It was Thursday, the week had been quite intense, and a walk on our trail would give us time to sort some things out. A walk on our trail is always good even if we don't have things to sort out.

When I arrived, I was delighted to see Adam, our twenty-month-old grandson, out on the driveway, "helping" his Dad with some spray painting. Daughter-in-law Sonja and grandson Ben were outside too. It felt great to be home. Grace came outside to join us, and we had a little visit before Grace and I started on our walk. We had not gone far when we heard Adam coming behind us. We turned and couldn't resist offering to take him on our walk. Sonja and Ben, bundled up in his snuggly, joined us too. Of course, this meant that our pace was delightfully slower than usual. We stopped to ponder the many mushrooms in our field that had sprung up literally overnight.

With the exception of the trail running through it, the grass in the field was eight to ten inches long and very wet from the recent downpours. Adam decided to cut across the field, following his curiosity. I followed him to see what he was interested in. He paused for a moment and studied the ever-growing pile of branches and tree trunks that had been gathered over the summer for winter wood fires.

I walked past Adam, inviting him to take a look at the pond with me. When I was about twenty feet ahead of him, I turned around to see him standing stationary in the same spot. He looked at me and spoke his personal universal "word" to get my attention. It was hard work for him to push his little legs through the matted grass, and he wanted my help. A broad smile crossed his face as he reached out with both of his arms towards me. He stayed where he was, certain that I would respond to him, and of course I did.

It was a magical moment for Grandpa. I walked towards the spot where he was stuck and let his arms wrap around my head. I lifted him to my chest, and off we went. It had been a place of struggle for him, but not for me. Maybe someday our roles will be reversed.

I thought of a Bible verse that seemed appropriate (Isaiah 46:4): "I will be your God throughout your lifetime—until your hair is white with age. I made you, and I will care for you. I will carry you along and save you."

Remembrance Day

"This is a day to remember forever—the day you left Egypt,
the place of your slavery. Today the LORD has brought you
out by the power of his mighty hand." – Exodus 13:3

"Always remember that Jesus Christ, a descendant
of King David, was raised from the dead.
This is the Good News I preach."
– 2 Timothy 2:8

I awoke to the promise of a fabulous sunrise on the eleventh day of November. A thin red line traced the mountaintops east of our home. In the grayness of dawn, I could see that the sunrise would be short lived, and I hoped that all would be still as I waited for the sacredness of dawn.

As I sat at our kitchen table with a cup of coffee in my hand, I thought of the many who had given their lives in the two world wars and the many other wars that seem to plague our existence. It was Remembrance Day, Memorial Day in other countries, a day to remember those who died tragically in the service of their country. What horrors did they experience?

I have never known anyone personally who was killed in war, but many of our elderly residents within our Hallmark Retirement Communities were in the military during World War Two. There are fewer now than when we opened thirteen years ago. I have heard some of their stories and seen the hollowness in their eyes that makes me wonder what else they have had to live with as a result of their service to our country.

As I sat in the stillness of the morning, in the comfort of my home, I found comprehension impossible. Losses on all sides of war make one wonder what "winning" a war really means, if there is such a thing. I have no answers at all, but I am grateful for the freedoms that we take for granted. They did not come for free. I wish there did not have to be war, as I am sure most of us do, and yet it seems that we have grown accustomed to live with violence.

I knew that our son Jared and his wife Sonja would be laying a wreath at the local cenotaph, along with other members of her family. They would be doing this on behalf of her father, who was returning from his duties as Minister of International Trade later in the day. I also knew that our son Ryan would be participating in a Remembrance Day parade as a firefighter in his community of 100 Mile House. I wondered if we should attend the local ceremony. I almost felt ashamed that we had lived in this community for over thirty years and had never yet attended it. Grace expressed her willingness to attend as well.

What is a cenotaph? I should know by now at my age. I know what it is physically, but what does the word mean? I discovered today that the word has Greek roots and refers to an empty tomb—a memorial for those who have died elsewhere.

If the tomb was empty, Thunderbird Square around the cenotaph certainly was not today. We were very moved by the thousands in attendance. Red poppies were the common ground outside, and a need to be together the common ground inside. There was soberness in the air. A military plane flew overhead, its appearance bringing a noticeable hush to the crowd. The crowd was multinational, likely including representatives from many sides of world conflicts.

The ceremony was very well orchestrated. The playing of "The Last Post" brought tears to many. This call by a lone bugle was used over a hundred years ago to call wounded and lost troops back to camp, marking the end of battle for the day. It meant they could come "home" and rest. Apparently, it is used now to symbolically beckon the spirits of soldiers lost overseas to return to their home communities. Then came the two minutes of silence, one to remember the dead, and the second to remember the grieving.

Shortly after the silence, a military officer proceeded to read a roll call of the ones from our community who had been killed in action, name after name from World War One. Another official responded to the roll call, announcing that none had answered. A similar roll call was made for the killed from other wars, with the same response of "No answer." One from our area had been killed in the recent war in Afghanistan. Grace and I stood near his mother, his wife, and his young daughter. I can't imagine being his mother, wife, or child, hearing his name called, and hearing no answer.

We are grateful that we went to the ceremony today. I have felt a bit subdued ever since—as perhaps I should. Silently, I joined the military chaplain as he gave a beautiful prayer, including a request for peace. I must realize that if there is ever going to be peace, it has to start in me. I must become the peace that I want to see in the world.

It was our first Remembrance Day ceremony, but one that will have a lasting impact on us. I felt a new sense of appreciation for the many among us who gave what we consider to be the ultimate sacrifice.

I am grateful for the gift of salvation that bridges the unexplainable, breaks through the suffering and violence, and points us to love. Therein lies an answer to all of this—and yet why is religion, ours included, seemingly at the heart of so much conflict?

I pray that I will be part of the peace that this world needs so desperately.

As I had anticipated, the sunrise was spectacular, but very short lived.

Carving My Life

"Many believe—and I believe—that I have been designated for this work by God. In spite of my old (not yet for me) age, I do not want to give it up; I work out of love for God and I put all my hope in him." – Michelangelo

Over the years, I have enjoyed watching wood carvers as they have used specialized tools to turn a log into a beautiful object—or, as many of them would say, "to find out what is inside the log and bring it to life." Some talk of the importance of "listening" to the log before starting and then being mindful that the carving is actually a journey of discovery to see what is contained therein. Michelangelo said, "Every block of stone has a statue inside it, and it is the task of the sculptor to discover it." As the carver or sculptor draws closer to that "statue," I imagine that each successive chisel cut requires more thought and deliberateness. As the statue nears completion, more time is required to decide what goes and what stays.

I wonder if there is something in there for me as I age and hopefully become closer to what God intended me to be. One of our wise elderly residents at Hallmark Retirement Communities commented that as she aged, her journey narrowed. I understand more and more what she meant.

I am very grateful for the life I have been given, even though there have been lots of challenges and I am sure there are many more ahead. I used to want to know more about my future, as impossible as that is. Now I don't think I do as much. I am in a different time of life. I know who holds the future, and I am learning to trust that

Jesus will "bring me safely home to God" (I Peter 3:18).

When I was younger, it wasn't nearly as difficult (or at least so it seemed) to determine what was good for me and what wasn't. It seemed that no end of opportunities came my way. I sampled much—some things seemed to fit, and some not so well—but I just carried on, leaving behind what didn't fit. Perhaps it was like stripping away the "bark and first large chunks of wood" in the carving out of my life. Now it seems that when I have to chisel something away, I often have to choose between what's good and what's best—the decisions are much harder. I am grateful that God, family, and friends help me with those decisions. It is as if I am getting closer to the center, closer to the "me" that God created, and thus it is more difficult to decide what to leave behind and what to keep. I find making decisions more challenging as I realize the potential impact of each decision on those around me whom I love. I hope to serve faithfully with what has been entrusted to me. I wonder why it seems to have taken so many years for me to get close to what I am supposed to be. Maybe I am a slow learner, or maybe that is just the way life is. As I continue my journey home, I am encouraged by the thought that "I am not alone because the Father is with me" (John 16:32).

Blue Bagging It

"Don't store up treasures here on earth, where moths eat them and rust destroys them, and where thieves break in and steal. Store your treasures in heaven, where moths and rust cannot destroy, and thieves do not break in and steal. Wherever your treasure is, there the desires of your heart will also be." – Matthew 6:19-21

"Take delight in the LORD, and he will give you your heart's desires." – Psalm 37:4

The bifold doors of the closet in my office are known to spring open frequently under protest because of the piles of minutes, notes, binders, bills, financial statements, and other records that have been stored there over the twenty plus years that we have lived here. Rather than disturb the contents, I have chosen to let sleeping dogs (and documents) lie and have proceeded to pile subsequent paperwork on the floor of my office or stuff it into the shelves of my bookcase. The latter practice has caused piles of books to gather on every other flat surface in my office, barely leaving enough room on my desk for me to write.

Well, today I decided to do something about it. That thought had occurred to me on numerous previous occasions, but today would be different.

I did not give myself time to answer the question "Where do I start?" knowing full well that that would repeat the same mistake I have made on several previous attempts.

I squatted down beside a pile of documents next to my desk.

It would not take long in this position before my legs would be asleep. I grabbed an armful of papers, placed them on my lap, and started to leaf through the first few pages. I found them quite entertaining, and I often paused to read a bit. I would not have kept anything that was unimportant, so why not enjoy the read? A brochure from a recent Abbotsford Community Foundation event, where I had served for nine years, was quite interesting, as was information on the Discovery Trails recently constructed in our community.

Then I came to my senses. The feeling in my legs was already almost gone, and I realized that, at this pace, my legs would have atrophied before I got through this first stack. The papers on my lap represented only six inches of an eighteen-inch pile, and there were more piles after this one was taken care of.

By now, Grace was quite excited. She had been challenging me for the last six years to clean up my piles of paper. She decided to help me cull the stack and make sure that whatever needed shredding was pushed sheet by sheet through our shredder.

The bar for shredding eligibility was lowered faster than the time it took my legs to fall asleep. Reams of files and budgets were indiscriminately dropped into a blue bag for recycling. I have no idea if there is a weight restriction for each bag in order to not overburden the fellow picking up the recyclables at the road—I guess I will find out later this week when he comes to pick them up.

As I flipped through the pages, I kept guard to make sure no vestige of sentimentality was allowed to hinder the discarding process. But I realized that easily a hundred thousand dollars of time had been spent on the pile of paper that I was now carelessly dropping into the blue bags. This information had been very important to me and many others at one time. The contents had helped shape some good—and perhaps some not so good—decisions and outcomes over the years. They represented a lot of hard work and much hard-won understanding.

I used to pride myself on reading through as much pertinent information as I could for the boards and committees that I served on over the years. Where did all of those words go? No wonder my head is tired and today I would rather read children's stories to our grandkids.

I know that I can't take it with me—as fundraisers are eager to remind me—but will I take some of it with me? Has all of this work shaped my life, and will it affect my eternal life? Or will I drop everything I have learned and start fresh when I pass on from this earth? Had the lack of blood circulation in my bent legs also reduced the blood flow to my brain? Is that what had caused me to entertain such a thought?

I continued to plow through the piles and files, but a sense of loss started to creep in from somewhere. Knowing what that could lead to, I expedited the clearing of the last stack that I had hoped to tackle today, carried the bags downstairs, and put them in the garage to await garbage day.

In less than three hours, I had thrown away hundreds of hours of reading and study and countless ideas eagerly shared by those involved. Had my values changed that much?

I think not. I had simply had to accept the reality that I must downsize. Grace has been painstakingly working at reducing her possessions for some time. Now it was time for me to do my part. There was no point in waiting any longer for moths to make lunch out of my stuff or a thief to break in and steal it. I would have to take care of this burden myself.

The information I had stored was not of no value. It was important, and is important, but I cannot keep storing stuff—unless I can figure out how to get it to heaven, where I should have a lot more time to sort through the piles. Until then, I guess I will just have to keep purging. The closet still needs attention.

I noticed, though, that some stuff is likely not leaving this house without me.

I have a gingerbread picture frame on my desk. I am very surprised that the moths and even our cat have not sampled it. It has been on my desk for over four years. Why do I keep it? Because it has a picture of my granddaughter in it. It is representative of the next generation, part of our legacy, a reminder of what is important, as I work at my desk.

I have two pictures of Grace on the wall in front of my desk.

One is of her in a sunflower field in the prairies, taken about fifteen years ago. The other is a more recent one.

I have a well-used Bible with tiny print that I read just about every morning. Instead of replacing it with a larger print version, which is readily available on the bookshelves beside me, I use reading glasses to read the well-marked pages over and over again.

I have most of a shelf full of journals, written over the last ten to fifteen years—of what value will they be? They are full of pictures of our family, stories of our family, stories of our friends—our story. They will likely be one of the last things to go. Their contents are not nearly as profound as the files now lying in the garage, but to me, they are beyond price.

I am often blown away at how important writing seems to be to me. Why do I get up every morning and feel a need to write? I have many reasons: I enjoy it. No one other than myself has any expectations from it. It helps me remember. It forces me to pause and learn more fully. But, at times, it seems deeper than that.

I guess I will just keep filling the shelves with journals and move whatever I have to in order to make room for them—because the desire to write seems to be intensifying.

Alone

*"Then the LORD God said, 'It is not good
for the man to be alone. I will make
a helper who is just right
for him.'" – Genesis 2:18*

*"Be happy with what you have. God has
said, 'I will never leave you or let you
be alone.'" – Hebrews 13:5 NLV*

It was a rainy, cold Sunday morning. Grace was not feeling well. We had stayed home from church the previous night, our normal time for attending, because of her cold, and it looked like she would not be going this morning either.

I wanted to attend church, but I was more than willing to stay home, as quiet mornings are very rare and equally as precious to me. Our son Jared needed a ride to church, where he would be meeting his girlfriend. I could have just dropped him off and returned home, but, for whatever reason, I decided to attend church at the same time.

My normal life requires that I do a lot of what I do without Grace. We are very busy in our own worlds, but we share quite a bit as well. We have always shared going to church. In fact, I probably can count on one hand the number of times that I have gone to church without her in over thirty-five years of marriage. I confess that I was uncertain about attending by myself, but I found a little comfort in knowing that Jared would be there as well.

The feelings I had were ridiculous, especially in an "independent, secure, confident," middle-aged man. The feelings were under the surface, and I could keep them in check without a problem, but, for experimental purposes, I decided to allow them to surface. I knew several people who had lost a spouse and who continued to attend our church. I have often wondered what that would feel like.

Well, I got a tiny taste of it that day and came away grateful that it was only temporary.

Entering the church, I did not know if I should wait for Jared and his girlfriend Sonja or go sit by myself. A tiny bit of insecurity stepped in, once again easily dispelled. I stood by Jared in the entrance, and then walked across to the bulletin boards to busy myself until Sonja arrived. I did not want to be a bother to them, an unwanted extra person clinging to them. I thought it weird that I would even think that. Jared was my son.

I had understood that Sonja's family might have saved a place for them, I was quite willing to sit by myself, but I must admit that I was relieved when I heard them discuss the matter and decide to sit with me. We sat in the very back row of the church, the only place where we could find three seats together.

I had no trouble finding my comfortable self. This was my church. I was familiar with this place. There were lots of wonderful friends around me. I settled in to embrace the service.

And then we prayed. Grace and I have always held hands when we pray. Inadvertently, I almost reached out for Jared's hand, as he was sitting beside me. I then realized how alone I felt in that moment, and my heart went out to the many for whom this is not a temporary experience.

We moved into the worship component of the service, singing familiar songs. I often take Grace's hand as we stand to sing if the song is particularly meaningful or it speaks to a shared part of our life. At times, we stand in silence, unable to sing the words. We do not need to talk—we stand there as two people sharing the journey, holding each other up. But today I stood alone.

Yes, I was beside one of our sons, but he will travel along his pathway to wherever it takes him. Our sons will be there for us—I know that—but that is different from having someone constantly at my side.

How many are there among us who feel that sense of aloneness every day? I only got a taste of it, but for a moment there was a real sense of being alone. Someday that may happen to me, or to Grace.

I tried to envision sitting there alone every Sunday. Would my friends still greet me, or would they pass by, not knowing how to engage with me? I have steered away from a widower in our church from time to time, fearing a long conversation. Oh, I have talked to him as well at other times, but not always.

How many among us are lonely? Does their loneliness speak to us and amplify our fear of being alone—or of being lonely, since there is a vast difference between the two? I can't imagine what it would be like to be left alone in this world, which is so full of busyness. Many in our eldercare homes live that way. When they bow to pray at lunch, there is no hand to hold.

I am still a strong advocate of the value of having time alone, something that has become more and more important to me over the years. But I also got some insight into the loneliness of being left alone, and that was not a good feeling.

It was good to get home and have lunch with Grace—and hold her hand while praying.

Safe

*"For our present troubles
are small and won't last very long.
Yet they produce for us a glory
that vastly outweighs them
and will last forever!"*
– 2 Corinthians 4:17

*"In skating over thin ice,
our safety is in our speed."*
– Ralph Waldo Emerson

It was a sunny spring afternoon. Blossoming trees lined the streets throughout our community and welcomed me as I walked up the ramp into the care home to visit with a dear friend. Our regular meetings had been disrupted over the last month by a trip to see our kids up north and by a lingering seasonal cold—I thought it best to stay away until I was no longer contagious. It had come with a nasty cough, especially at night, robbing both Grace and me of sleep, since she had contracted it first. I had finally gotten through a night without a hacking spell. I hoped this qualified me to pay my friend a visit.

As I entered the home, I was struck by the growing circle of residents collected in the entrance lounge, facing a mostly muted TV. The majority looked asleep. The few who appeared to be awake hardly noticed my entrance. I offered a smile, expecting nothing in return—perhaps an indication of my ageism.

I went down the hallway to my friend's room. He was not in his chair. I wondered if he was out for the afternoon; if so, good for him. I noticed the bathroom door was closed. I tapped on it and heard his faint voice—he was present. To give him privacy, I stepped back into the hallway and waited. Knowing his condition, I was not sure how he would handle this situation. In a few minutes, an aide arrived to assist him. I wondered how long he had had to wait—his need not being critical and the staff in a place like this having more than enough tasks to fill a day.

We had a very meaningful visit, even though I often had to bend over as close as possible to try to hear his words and ask if my understanding was correct. I think he needed to talk. I needed to listen. The words we spoke would normally have taken twenty minutes to express. Today, they required an hour and a half. In his former life, my friend was known to be a fabulous communicator. He still is, but in a much different way. I have had to change the way I hear in order to appreciate what he says. Little by little, I think I am learning to listen.

Our talks always circle around God's love for us and the struggle to understand how that love is present in the midst of suffering. My friend has often told me that unless we suffer, we are unlikely to grow very much. Unfortunately, I think he is right.

I asked him what he would tell his as yet unborn first great-grandchild on the first day of school. I knew as I asked that it is very unlikely that he will be there to deliver the message in person. He said there were three things. The first was the gospel, the good news about Jesus' salvation. The second was how much Jesus loves him or her, using the story of Jesus blessing the little children. The third was how important our history is since "our past is important to our future."

I knew that during his early driving years, my friend had pushed a 1946 Chevy to over 100 miles per hour. I asked if he would tell his great-grandchild that too. He smirked and said, "I think all men have to drive over 100 miles per hour at least once in their lifetime." We had a good laugh. It was time for me to leave.

As I turned to leave, he extended his hand and asked if I would take hold of it. He wanted me to help him get up from his chair. I think he was hoping to walk me out of the building as he used to do on occasion. I did not see a walker anywhere and noticed that a fall alarm was attached to his shirt. Mentioning the alarm to him, I promised to send a staff member to assist him. Then I turned and walked down the hall towards the main exit and the beautiful fresh afternoon air, leaving him behind once again.

As I approached the door, two elderly ladies noticed and made a bolt for the door, hoping that if they moved fast enough, they could get out of this place too. I turned to prevent their exit. Two staff members intercepted them and redirected them back inside, in spite of their protests. They would have been far from safe outside on their own. But I wonder how safe they felt inside.

These visits cause me to think about the future for many I love. They cause me to think about what might be ahead for Grace and me too. Those are sobering thoughts. I drove home, very appreciative of what life allows me today.

The Last One at the Table

"Teach us to realize the brevity of life, so that we may grow in wisdom." – Psalm 90:12

"Elijah replied, 'I have zealously served the LORD God Almighty. But the people of Israel have broken their covenant with you, torn down your altars, and killed every one of your prophets. I am the only one left, and now they are trying to kill me, too." – 1 Kings 19:10

Over the years, I have enjoyed many meals within the Hallmark Retirement Communities. To sit at a table with a collection of the elderly, each one a treasure trove of life experience, is indeed a privilege. Story after story spills out at random, and laughter and tears blend with one another.

I have watched, too, as residents develop very close friendships within our communities. They chatter with one another as they file into the dining room. But don't let that apparent good humor lead you to make the mistake of challenging the perceived ownership of a particular seat in the dining room. It doesn't happen often fortunately, but on occasion an unknowing "newbie" has been informed: "You cannot sit there. That seat is for _____." And the offending individual is summarily sent off to seek out a safer place. It can be heartbreaking. I hope that if I live long enough, I will not forget what I have observed and I will extend more grace to others around me.

I have also observed those same close friendships continue at the table. Some tables have lively discussions. At others, the residents allow each other silence and comfort. Typically, the same group collects at a given table each mealtime. We are no different from people from many other cultures who gather around food for friendship and communion.

I have also watched as one member of a certain "table community" is absent from his or her chair for one meal, and then another meal, and then longer. The others at the table know what is going on. I can hardly imagine the sense of loss that must creep in when that friend does not show up once again.

And then, one day, a single rose and a picture announce that the friend is gone and will not be returning. At lunchtime, he is missing.

Perhaps then the experience around the table might be expressed like this:

There is silence at our table, uncomfortable at first, but then we talk again. We talk a little about our friend. I fight back tears and promise not to become as attached again—this is too painful. I look up at those sitting with me. It is too late, they are already my friends, but I will not allow this to happen with any new person who joins this table. I will be civil but guard my heart. We are all in our eighties. How long can we live? Why become friends?

A week later, a shock settles on all of us around the table. Another one of our friends is missing. The word has quickly spread in the community that she died of a heart attack last night. Of all those at our table, I would have expected that she would outlive us all. I guess I was wrong. Now there are only four of the original six of us—no one fills either of the two chairs. I guess we will carry on.

A month later, failing health afflicts one of the remaining four. The "assessment" requires that this gentleman move to a community that provides higher levels of care. I bet that he would rather stay here since we care for him, but he really has no choice.

Now we are down to three. Conversation is much sparser these days. I feel as if we have withdrawn from one another. We are saying goodbye to the living. My neighbors, my friends, are alive, but I feel that they are slipping away—or is it I who am slipping away?

I notice the lady beside me. I used to call her Susan, but Susan seems to have become lost. Susan is gone, I think. I do not remember when she left, but the lady beside me no longer talks at all. She sits pleasantly beside me, but she no longer asks about my day. She no longer talks about her children or complains about aches and pains. I even miss that part of our conversation. She picks at her food as if dissecting it to find a treasure that she believes is in there somewhere.

Today, she did not show up. I do not know if I want to know anything more than that. Now we are two. We don't even look at one another. I glance her way but quickly turn back to my plate of food. We sit in silence as if waiting, waiting to see who will be the last one at the table.

Joy and Sorrow

"Shared joy is twice the joy.
Shared sorrow is half the sorrow."

"You keep track of all my sorrows.
You have collected all my tears
in your bottle. You have recorded
each one in your book."
– Psalm 56:8

I met her as she pushed her walker up to her door, key in hand. She is another one of our beautiful residents. I had heard that she had not been feeling that well lately and felt our friendship gave permission to enquire.

She, in a quivering voice, said, "Not bad, but always lots of little pains." She then went on to say how thankful she was to live within our community—deflecting her short report on her current health and choosing to speak of joy.

I told her about a Swedish proverb that states, "Shared joy is twice the joy. Shared sorrow is half the sorrow."

She stepped toward me and gave me a hug. Then, touching her left chest, she said that she had sorrow in there. Moving her hand to the right side, she told me that she had joy in there. She teared up and apologized for her emotional state. She said that she often has to retreat to her suite to be in private because her emotions can swing wildly and unpredictably. She lost a grandson a few years ago in a tragic accident. I would think there is more, of course, at her age, but she also exudes a deep joy.

Joy and sorrow co-exist in us all. A good friend, suffering with

Parkinson's disease, told me that without suffering, he doubts that we would grow much as people. He then added that he really doesn't feel that he has suffered much compared to many. On the surface, there would be plenty of reason to disagree with him in his condition. Perhaps, without joy we would not know suffering, and without suffering we would not know joy. So maybe we have to be willing to accept them both in our life and see that the suffering, perhaps inexplicably, is a gift as well.

Corrected Vision and a Good Day

*"I pray that the eyes of your heart may be enlightened
in order that you may know the hope to which he has
called you, the riches of his glorious inheritance."
– Ephesians 1:18 NIV*

*"Death and love are the two wings that bear
the good person to heaven." – Michelangelo*

A couple of days ago, the Executive Director of Hallmark Retirement Communities met one of our residents in the hallway. It was first thing in the morning. He greeted her as usual, but her response was not normal, at least for her. Although there is plenty of evidence that she is overshadowed by a degree of dementia, she is always cordial, offering a smile and a friendly greeting to everyone she meets. On this morning, uncharacteristically, she said that she was not doing so well. Then she added: "I can't see very well." Fortunately, our Executive Director noticed the problem right away and suggested that she needed to put her glasses on. In a minute, she returned, as happy as ever, wearing her glasses. She had forgotten that she wore glasses.

That is understandable, but also quite profound. I wonder how often the rest of us live without "glasses" on as well. I have no idea why, but some mornings, and especially some evenings, I can't seem to "see" too clearly either. Maybe I have received too much tough news during the day or I have wrestled with too many troubling thoughts at night, and I have forgotten to put on the "glasses" of knowing I am loved. Maybe someday God will finish His surgery on my eyes, and I will not need a reminder. But maybe that is exactly the way it is supposed to be today.

This Christmas season, I have been thinking about what prophetic message the people heard before Jesus' arrival. The Israelites had lived under constant oppression and were hoping for better times. I suspect that what they really wanted was to stop being the oppressed and to return to being the oppressor, as had been the case at times in the Old Testament. When God had seemed to be on their side, they had gotten carried away, and the pendulum of justice had quickly swung past the center point. The Israelites wanted a king to deliver them from suffering, but I think also to provide a special status to their culture, to their identity as God's chosen people.

Then Jesus came along—born of a virgin in a barn—and they were told that this was the promised Messiah. They even provided Him with a royal entry parade into Jerusalem, hoping that their plight was finally about to change. A few days later, those hopes were dashed on a cruel cross. Jesus, who had healed many and raised others from the dead, who had claimed to be Deity, seemed helpless before a mob. A mob composed of his own race, the Jews, and those ruling over them, the Romans, joined forces to put Him to death. Profound bewilderment must have been mixed in with grief. His followers were not yet able to understand Jesus' previous warning that He must die.

And then, on the third day, it all changed, and new "glasses" appeared. This Messiah rose again, achieving victory over death. He healed the rift between God and humans, a chasm that could not be crossed any other way. Try as we might, on the other side of that chasm, we humans were incapable of establishing a Kingdom that would meet our longing. Until Christ healed our hearts and restored that most wonderful relationship with God the Father, we could not put the right glasses on. This new Kingdom would resonate within the depths of our hearts, we would taste "home"—and we would start to see each other differently. We would see that we are all in this together—loved and being loved, leaving room for one another, and no longer feeling the need to oppress others and force them to conform to our way. If we wear those "glasses," we might just have a chance of seeing with corrected eyes. Perhaps then we could love one another and allow ourselves to be loved. Now, that is Good News!

A Soft Heart

*"He comforts us in all our troubles so that we
can comfort others. When they are troubled, we
will be able to give them the same comfort
God has given us." – 2 Corinthians 1:4*

*"While he was still a long way off, his father saw
him coming. Filled with love and compassion, he
ran to his son, embraced him, and kissed him."
– Luke 15:20*

*"When death, the great reconciler has come,
it is never our tenderness we repent of,
but our severity." – George Eliot*

"Live life"—together, those two words indicate a desire to be
alive, to show up, to feel, to be loved, etc. But I wonder if there
is a temptation for us to instead move towards a "hardened life."
Rather than living a strong life rich with feeling, we may think
that living a strong life requires "toughness." Challenges face us
all. There is unspeakable violence all around us, leading us to
wonder if the shadow of hatred exists in our own hearts as well.
To protect myself from being swallowed up, I can develop healthy
boundaries—and I do. But I can also protect myself by becoming
hardened. The busyness of life, the thirst for fulfillment, the desire
for acceptance—these can all become barriers between me and
God, subconsciously hardening my heart towards Him and others.
At that point, I am lost, left to my own pursuits.

And yet God comes to live among us, in our mess, and to suffer as we do. In doing so, He also shows us a way, a path home. He comes in the most humble of ways, as a baby in a manger, helpless, dependent on others for survival. That is a priceless gift to us all. I pray that I will remain tender to that reality in the midst of the suffocating busyness of the Christmas season.

Mark 6:45-52 tells the story of Jesus walking on a stormy lake in the middle of the night to where the disciples were in serious trouble. Jesus had, on the previous day, miraculously fed the multitudes—five thousand men and their families—with an ample meal of fish and loaves of bread. Jesus sent the disciples across the lake that evening, knowing that they would get caught up in a storm. In the meantime, He went up into the hills by Himself to pray. Jesus saw the trouble the disciples were in, and at three o'clock in the morning He headed out, walking on the stormy lake in their direction. He was apparently intending to go past them (verse 48). But when they cried out in fear, thinking he was a ghost, He spoke to them: "Don't be afraid. Take courage. I am here!" (verse 50) Those are words that I would like to hear today. Then Jesus climbed into the boat, and the wind stopped. Verses 51-52 record that the disciples were totally amazed, "for they still didn't understand the significance of the miracle of the loaves. Their hearts were too hard to take it in." By now, the disciples had witnessed numerous miracles, including healings and the incredible provision of food for thousands, and yet their hearts were too hard to take it in. That sobers me. I fear that I, too, belong to that camp of people with hardened hearts.

As I get closer to my elder years, I often pray for a tender heart. Tenderness can leave my heart broken, and yet I pray that that is the path I am on. Tenderness is far from weakness. God demonstrates His tenderness toward us in countless ways. I hope I miss fewer of them and I learn to extend tenderness to those around me as well.

Facing Our Fears

*"Don't be afraid, for I am with you.
Don't be discouraged, for I am your God.
I will strengthen you and help you.
I will hold you up with my victorious
right hand." – Isaiah 41:10*

We have one of those delightful Christmas nutcrackers. He stands about sixteen inches tall, including his fuzzy Cossack hat. We bring him out every Christmas, and, for almost a month, he stands guard, looking stately. He is mostly decorative. But, at times, we will use the lever on his back to crush a peanut shell between his jaws and munch on the freed contents.

This Christmas, we brought him out as usual and introduced him to Adam, our 22-month-old grandson. We thought nothing of it, but Adam was not at all impressed. To the contrary, he was visibly offended by the nutcracker's presence in our familiar home. He pointed at it and whimpered. This initially surprised us, but we did eventually catch on and followed his direction to rid the room of the intruder. As Adam watched, we put the nutcracker in the closet under the stairs off our living room and closed the door. He eyed the door carefully to make sure that there was no likelihood of escape and then carried on.

But he was wary every time he came to our home. At times, he would pause and point at the closed door separating him from the intruder. It eventually became clear to us that he was wanting to look in the closet and make sure that the nutcracker was not hiding somewhere else. I picked Adam up so he could take a closer look at the nutcracker standing on a top shelf. He was interested in a closer look—but not too close.

A couple of days ago, upon his arrival, he went right to the closed door and indicated that he wanted to take another look at the nutcracker. He pointed at the door and then tapped two fingers on his open hand. It made a tapping sound—the sound of the nutcracker.

We opened the door and placed the nutcracker down on the floor. Adam stood close to the nutcracker, but still inches away, watching intently. I encouraged him to touch the fuzzy hat. He did, but immediately jerked his hand away. So, we put the nutcracker away again and hoped that perhaps next year it would be different.

But the next time Adam came over, he wanted to see the nutcracker again. By then, Grace had put him away for the year. Adam continued to petition, so we all went upstairs and dug the nutcracker out of the storage area. Adam wasn't finished with him yet. We returned the nutcracker to his place under the stairs, where Adam seemed to be satisfied with him being—for now.

The next day, Grace was to take care of Adam, and Adam made it clear to her that he wanted to see the nutcracker again. By the time I got home, things had changed. They were now friends!

Fear is not only the enemy of toddlers. It can grip adults too. Fear of the unknown is perhaps one of the most common sources of our anxiety. What lies ahead? What happens if...? What about...? The questions are innumerable.

One of the most unanswerable questions is about death itself. We can try to hide it under the stairs, as we did with the nutcracker for Adam. But, as we age, our curiosity will likely cause us to think about it more and more. I know I certainly do. I suppose working with elderly folks for many years has helped inform my interest. On more than one occasion, I have heard a resident say, "It is not death that I fear, but the way of dying." That makes good sense to me.

What I cling to on my journey "home" is a little nugget found in 1 Peter 3:18: "Christ suffered for our sins once for all time. He never sinned, but he died for sinners to bring you safely home to God." I will trust in that assurance, knowing that I will get safely home. I am in very good hands.

CPSIA information can be obtained
at www.ICGtesting.com
Printed in the USA
LVOW06s0854021216
515390LV00005B/6/P